THROUGH THE KEYHOLE

SOLVING THE COLD CASE OF LORETTA JONES

SHAWNEE BARNES

TWELVE TUESDAYS
PUBLISHING

THROUGH THE KEYHOLE

This is a work of non-fiction providing historical information about the subjects discussed. The author has recreated events, relationships, and conversations based on public records, news articles, and interviews with involved parties. In order to maintain the privacy of some individuals, their names, physical characteristics, occupations, or places of residence may have been changed, as noted with an asterisk*. Although the publisher and author have made every effort to ensure that the information was correct at press time, no express or implied warranties or guarantees are expressed or implied by their choice of content. The publisher and author assume no responsibility for errors, inaccuracies, omissions, or any other inconsistencies and shall not be held liable or responsible to any person or entity with respect to any incidental or consequential damages alleged to have been caused, directly or indirectly, by the information contained herein.

Library of Congress Control Number: 2024905541

First Paperback Edition July 2024

Cover Design by Shawnee Barnes
Cover Photo by Mauricio Umana
Author Photo by Shailee Stokes Photography
Book Design and Typesetting by Enchanted Ink Publishing
Editing by Enchanted Ink Publishing

The text type was set in Palatino Linotype

ISBN: 979-8-9885321-1-8 (e-Book)
ISBN: 979-8-9885321-0-1 (Paperback)

Twelve Tuesdays Publishing, LLC

TWELVE TUESDAYS
PUBLISHING

304 S. Jones Blvd #4232
Las Vegas, NV 89107
www.12twelvetuesdays.com

Dedicated to Loretta and Heidi:

Mother and Daughter Heroes

AUTHOR'S NOTE

Many people have asked how I came to be the author of this book. It all started with a chance encounter and a shared passion for justice and storytelling.

I had just returned from a two-week writing course in Ireland and was sitting in the quiet corner of my newly remodeled attic admiring my vintage "clickety-clack" typewriter when I heard a knock on my door. Little did I know that the knock and this typewriter would soon play a pivotal role in the creation of a book about a forty-six-year-old cold case.

Two Carbon County sheriff's deputies stood on the porch of my grandparents' old coal-mining house, now my second home, to inquire about an animal control situation. I invited them in, and over coffee and cinnamon rolls, we discussed shared connections between law enforcement and the community. Sergeant David Brewer noticed the typewriter and was curious about its purpose. When I mentioned my intention to write a book, he shared the intriguing story of the cold case that he and the victim's daughter, Heidi Jones-Asay, had solved and asked if I'd be interested in putting it on paper.

With a background in criminal justice and a passion for true crime, I was drawn to the challenge of unraveling the mysteries surrounding Loretta Jones's tragic fate. My upbringing in Carbon and Emery counties in the seventies provided insight into the small-town dynamics and complexities that influenced the case.

When Heidi and I met later that month at a local coffee shop, we quickly realized our intertwined connections through mutual friends and family. We agreed I should write their book, and two years later, it was finally completed.

Me, Myself and I

Poem written by Loretta Jones, September 28, 1963

A person has three people really . . . me, myself & I.

And not everybody meets all three.

If I like someone I normally let them know I

And some meet me

I don't let many people meet myself.

Myself is someone special.

I only show myself to people I really care about.

Me hasn't much say-so in anything

because Me keeps still.

People say I have a split personality,

everyone does.

There are really three people in every one person.

So for every two people in a class there are really six.

If someone says be yourself

Say, myself is special

I wish to be me.

FOREWORD

Through the Keyhole

Rachel H. Walton

Set in the small rural coal-mining town of Price, Utah, *Through the Keyhole* takes place during the halcyon days of the late 1960s and early 1970s. It is a compelling and haunting narrative about four-year-old Heidi Jones. One morning in July 1970, she awakened and looked through the keyhole of her bedroom door to see her twenty-three-year-old unwed mother lying dead in a pool of blood on the living room floor.

It is a deeply introspective chronicle detailing her decades-long quest to bring her mother's killer to justice and the initial uncertainty of not knowing who the killer was. These pages offer a window into a more tranquil time in America's past, an idyllic time when children played safely in the streets, neighbors knew one another, and people did not lock their doors. In a sense, however, this is a love story. While it is the story of a daughter's love for her mother, whom she had only begun to know, it is also the story of a young mother's love for her daughter—a young mother who, in her final death throes, wrote her killer's name in blood on the floor as she struggled to save her little girl from a similar fate by remaining silent.

In the pages that follow, the author paints a heart-wrenching picture of the impact of this case on Heidi's life and soul as the crime went unresolved for over forty years. A *cold case murder*. Through the delicate brushstrokes of words, Loretta Jones comes back to life in this chronicle, which spans decades. We experience the time, the place, and the family and community dynamics surrounding Loretta, who was a single mother raising her daughter in a deeply religious Mormon environment. In a sense, Loretta—a beautiful young woman who sought only the happiness and security of love and a family—did not die that Saturday night. Through the author's skillful narrative, she lives forever now as personal reflections of Heidi's youth and subsequent struggles with memories of her mother, intricately stitched and woven together as she seeks justice.

Cold case. A term deeply embedded today in the American lexicon, it is one much disliked by many investigators. To the average person, it is a murder that went unsolved, but to the families and friends of a murder victim, it sends a message that you have been forgotten and your case is not investigated. Strictly speaking, homicide is the killing of one human being by another and may be legally justified or excused from punishment. Murder, however, is the *unlawful* killing of one human being by another and carries severe legal consequences. The number of unsolved murders in the United States is unknown, but reliable estimates consider a quarter of a million persons not to be an unreasonable number. Small town. Big city. Murder knows no political or geographic boundaries. No race, gender, or economic status is immune.

Historically, larger jurisdictions with increased crime rates usually maintained specialized investigative units of experienced teams who responded to death investigations and established protocols for investigation and documentation of investigative efforts. Smaller policing agencies with few, if any, murders often did not. According to the National Institute of Justice, roughly 50 percent of American police agencies still have fifteen or fewer sworn officers. Death investigation is one in which experience counts. When a suspicious death occurs, it is too late to read a textbook or get classroom training. This is an arena where on-the-job training is the best teacher.

Into this unique field in criminal investigation steps the cold case investigator. In agencies without dedicated homicide units, personnel may be assigned to work such cases in addition to handling their regular day-to-day workload. Such was the experience of Sergeant David Brewer of the Carbon County Sheriff's Office. If these cases had been easy to solve, they would have been the first time. In an ideal world, when such investigations go unsolved, the files and evidence are boxed up and stored pending new investigative leads. Past practices, however, compound the problem for today's cold case homicide investigator. The bad guys never saw DNA coming, but neither did the good guys. Records and evidence were intentionally destroyed after a period of time due to a mindset that the case would never be solved. In other cases, files and evidence were lost or intentionally removed and disappeared. Such was Brewer's experience. In Loretta's case, the investigative record would have to be reconstructed from scratch.

Like the pattern in a beautifully woven Navajo rug, the author reveals the not-so-unusual public and personal struggles

Detective Brewer encountered during his seven-year investigation. While law enforcement offices see the worst and the best of humanity, they likewise are human beings. While some cops can leave the job behind after a day's work, dedicated officers such as Sergeant Brewer cannot. They live these investigations 24/7, 365 days a year. *Through the Keyhole* reveals the human toll these investigations can take on investigators as well. The author vividly portrays Detective Brewer's frustrations with the investigative process as well as his own internal personal struggles and self-doubts. These parallel narratives offer the reader profound awareness into the pains and frustrations experienced by survivors and investigators alike.

By this work, we gain deep insight into the impact the case had not only on Heidi's family and her community, but ultimately on the dedicated small-town ex-Marine-turned-sheriff's-detective who would not say *no* when it came to solving this cold case murder. These cases require a special type of investigator, and Brewer turned out to be the answer to Heidi's prayers.

Through the Keyhole is a masterpiece of drama, horror, injustice, and exploration of the lives of the daughter and the detective in a captivating must-read narrative. It is a source of inspiration for those whose cold cases remain unsolved. Every child survivor of such an event, as well as others in similar circumstances, should read this book. You are NOT alone in your struggles.

Rachel H. Walton, EdD
Author of *Cold Case Homicides: Practical Investigative Techniques*
Price, Utah
June 3, 2024

PROLOGUE

H opes dimmed as the noonday sun shone through the leaves of the big tree that towered over the freshly unearthed grave. Black water gushed as the backhoe lifted the casket vault from its forty-six-year-old home. The town gravedigger, who described the June day as "just plain creepy," had placed plenty of vaults into the ground, but this was the first time he had exhumed one. Equipment chains rattled and clunked as they carefully brought the heavy cement tomb out of its bed. The air smelled of dank grass and dirt. The rectangular box jerked and spun and suddenly tilted to one side, splashing liquid decay onto the shoes of those standing by. The body of twenty-three-year-old Loretta Jones had rested peacefully in this small Elmo, Utah, cemetery since 1970, and today's events aimed to expose her killer's identity. But the black water was not a good sign.

Heidi, now fifty years old, clung to the hand of her husband, Kevin. She let her mind take her back to the hand holding hers when she was four and standing next to the same grave. She remembered looking around, perplexed and curious, trying to make eye contact with her aunts and uncles for comfort. But their tears hindered the connection, and it scared her. She felt so small, and her grandmother's grip felt so tight. That day, the bright blue August sky starkly contrasted with the disquiet that consumed Heidi's young soul. Something was wrong. With eerie fascination, she watched as a delicate wooden casket, with her mother lying inside, was gently lowered into the ground. Heidi's small hand clung tightly to a rose. As she approached the coffin, her gaze fixed on the open abyss before her, she watched the family place their roses onto the box lid. Her grandmother helped her add her flower to the collection. Suddenly, she was turned away from the scene. And from her mother.

Today, determination replaced Heidi's confusion, and hope sprang eternal as the same wooden box came up from its grave.

Exhuming her mother's body was a painful decision Heidi had hoped to avoid. However, after running into nothing but brick walls in her mother's murder investigation, she felt driven to pursue this drastic measure. Despite years of striving to push the case forward, minimal progress was marked by frustration and setbacks.

As the gravediggers struggled to release the vault from the earth's deep grip, Heidi glanced at the marble headstone next to her mother's. Vergie LuDeen Jones, her grandmother, had died a year earlier, in 2015. A brief twinge of guilt surged through Heidi's body. She pushed it aside with a deep breath, determined not to let it sway her resolve. The decision to exhume her mother's body now rested solely with her—it was the last remaining avenue to pursue justice.

She looked up at Kevin. His reassuring grip on her hand provided a silent affirmation. With unwavering courage, Heidi remained steadfast in her conviction that this exhumation would unearth evidence crucial enough to expose a killer hiding in the shadows. Loretta's death had been too soon, and her killer had remained free for too long. This contrast was deeply painful for Heidi, which amplified her desire for closure and justice.

To others gathered around her, Heidi appeared confident and calm. Her mind, however, raced with what-ifs. What if there wasn't any DNA? What if time had reduced the odds of it being useful? What if this was a waste of time? But . . . What if it solved her mother's murder? That was the big *if* she was hoping for.

The same questions were being asked inside the minds of Carbon County Sheriff Sergeant David Brewer and other law enforcement officers who stood by to assist with the disinterment. Though circumstantial evidence for this case was piling up, most cases today were solved using scientific evidence, and in 1970, when Loretta was murdered, DNA testing did not exist. Could modern methods be used for Loretta's case?

Amid the memorable gathering, the most significant figure stationed by the graveside was a female reporter from ETV news. Her task was clear: to capture the details of the tragic event unfolding before her and broadcast the news as far as Colorado.

The vault was finally secured onto the back of a flatbed truck and transported, procession style, seventeen miles through the rural back roads of Elmo toward Price, Utah, where Loretta's body would sleep overnight in an auxiliary warehouse. The building had never held an unearthed coffin before, as exhumations were rare in this small town. But so were murders.

CHAPTER 1

MURDER IN A SMALL TOWN

Heat from the July sun turned the pavement into soft black tar. Vapor mirages danced upward, evaporating into the sky. High-pitched laughter permeated the muggy air as children gleefully darted between sparkling mists of cool water, their bare feet tickled by the thick green grass.

Clad in shorts, fathers tamed the flames of their smoky grills, coaxing seasoned flavors from sizzling burgers as they were flipped with expert precision and placed on paper plates in outstretched hands.

Under the warm rays of the sun, mothers moved about, carrying baskets of freshly laundered clothes to the clothesline. With care and affection, they pegged each garment onto the line, finding solace in the simple act of embracing the fresh air. A gentle hum escaped their lips as they worked, the rhythmic swaying of the clothes in the soothing breeze adding a harmonious melody to the serene atmosphere.

Typically brimming with school and work obligations, calendars now opened up to family picnics, where women secretly competed to showcase their best homemade pie or cake and children were free to run about ungoverned. Swimming parties at the local pool brought respite from the hot weather, and rodeos, those wild and dusty affairs, evoked spirits from the American West.

The soul found refuge in the unhurried pace of summer. There was a peculiar sensation as the hands of the clock seemed to hesitate a second longer, and breaths were drawn at full capacity. Time itself tended to slow in the idyllic summers of rural towns.

The silent sunset resonated the internal alarm for dinner, and kids scurried home on their bikes, tired and sweaty from a day spent playing in the dirt. Mother hung her apron up and finally rested among her family as they bowed their heads and gave thanks for the home-cooked meal.

As the day wound down, evening whispered in the sounds of a low train whistle and a lone dog barking in the distance. The ten o'clock news, asking if you knew where your children were, signed off for the day. No doors were locked, and windows stayed open to invite in the gentle night breeze.

This was not a place where bad things happened—that is, until that hot night in July when everyone's preconceived notions of this sleepy little town were awakened by the word *murder*.

The year was 1970, and the place was Price, Utah.

Price, located in west-central Carbon County, Utah, was settled in 1877 by a group of Mormon pioneers seeking land to expand their growing religion. Located in the Price River Valley, the town was named after William Price, a Mormon church bishop who discovered the river valley in 1869. The arrival of the Denver and Rio Grande Western Railroad in 1883 helped expand the town's population, increasing access to coal production, which became the bedrock for the growing economy, along with a dependence on livestock and agriculture like sugar beets and grains.

The Rio Grande Zephyr passenger train was introduced in 1970. Today, Amtrak's California Zephyr passes daily in each direction, with a station about seven miles away in another small Utah town, Helper.

With the completion of the railroad in 1883, the character of Price changed dramatically, transforming from an isolated farming community to the commercial hub of Castle Valley. The railroad was directly responsible for Price's evolution to the area's premier retail, political, educational, and cultural center.

The railroad created work opportunities for miners to access the nearby coal mines, and it wasn't long before thousands of foreign-born, non-Mormon immigrants found their way to the small community. Initially, they lived in coal camps near the mines, but eventually, Price opened its doors, welcoming immigrants from countries like Greece, Italy, Austria, and Japan. This assimilation made the city a cultural hub and reflects the current ethnic diversity of the county that remains to this day, making Price one of Utah's most culturally varied communities.

The immigrant population eventually introduced a variety of religions to the community, separating Price from neighboring communities primarily represented by Mormons. Carbon County had also historically voted Democratic, which was unique in heavily Republican-leaning Utah. This changed in 2010, when Carbon County elected its first Republican to Congress in almost seventy years and has since trended Republican.

But in 1970, traditional values still reigned supreme. For most of the children in Price, growing up in a small town resembled living in a fish bowl. Secrets didn't exist.

Days of the week mostly marked time, repeating the same daily routine of work and school. By Friday night, a need to release steam and crack open a beer came none too soon for the blue-collar workers. The younger crowd used their weekends to gather on Main Street and socialize, show off their cars, and flirt with the opposite sex.

Like most small towns, different groups existed: stoners, cowboys, jocks, and the goodie-two-shoes girls eager to meet more of their kind. Flirting might eventually lead to a malt at the corner Arctic Circle. A second date might include listening to Simon & Garfunkel's "Bridge over Troubled Water" while waiting for a movie to start at the outdoor drive-in, where actors' voices crackled from the speaker hanging inside your car window. But who actually watched the movie? Other kids would gather at Sherald's Burger Bar or Cooks Velvet Freeze drive-up window, popular hangouts where the servers came outside to take orders from your car and returned with corn dogs and Cokes, expertly balancing them on a metal tray they attached to your window. And if you wore a football jacket, you garnered some extra respect even during the summer. The letters on your jacket were chick magnets. Carbon High School had a winning football team. Overall, life was good for this provincial community.

However, on Thursday, July 30, 1970, while parents struggled to contain their teenagers' raging hormones and the mundane week was coming to an end, a distinct kind of drama unfolded in a quiet little house four blocks from the quaint main street.

Before that decisive date, Price was a safe place where children played outside alone, as with nine-year-old Lance Horvath, who sat in the dirt of his front yard the morning of July 31 digging for worms. Usually, this activity was shared with his next-door neighbor friend, Heidi, but this morning, she was late in joining him for their day's adventures. Around eleven, her front door opened, and Lance glanced up, shielding his eyes from the sun and wiping sweat from his forehead, to see the four-year-old slowly amble out of her house still in her nightgown.

Something about Heidi's face looked different. Her eyes were wide, and her skin was pale. She stood very still.

The night before had been typical for the single mother, Loretta, and her daughter, Heidi. Loretta had turned down an invitation from her sisters to join them on a trip to Moab, the small town near Arches National Park. She hoped that over the weekend, she would spend some time with Bob, the man she was dating. Being a weeknight, Loretta had to be at work the next morning, so an early dinner with just the two of them before Heidi was bathed and prepared for bed was the routine.

Loretta took great pride in her home. It was usual for the dinner dishes to be promptly washed and dried. As she performed this mundane task, her thoughts wandered to the man she longed to spend more time with: Bob. Managing as a single parent was a challenge she faced with resilience, but she couldn't help but yearn for companionship and the prospect of sharing her life with a soulmate. Was Bob the one she had been waiting for? The hopeful desire of the young, pretty mother was that he was indeed her man.

Before Loretta could tuck Heidi in for the evening, something happened that wasn't ordinary for a Thursday night. Evening darkened the room, and Loretta switched on the living room light. She intended to get Heidi to bed, read her a book, then change into her robe and watch a little TV. But a loud knock at the door changed her plans. Holding one of her favorite Little Golden Books, Heidi went to her bedroom and waited while her mother answered the door.

"Stay in your room, and don't come out," Loretta instructed Heidi when she finally entered the waiting child's bedroom. This was not part of the routine, Heidi thought. What about her bedtime story? Heidi put the book down and crawled in bed, wondering if she had upset her mother. She listened for her mother's footsteps outside the door in hopes she would come back in for a second kiss good night, but sleep overcame the perplexed child.

Groggy from a restless night, Heidi woke much later than usual. Her mother had not called her for breakfast. Was she expected to stay in her room until her mother beckoned her, or did that instruction only apply last night? Heidi was mixed up, so she chose to obediently stay in her bedroom, playing half-heartedly with her toys. Her growling stomach prompted her to go to the door, where she stood and listened. When she heard no sign of her mother in the next room, she peered through the keyhole of her bedroom door. She saw what looked like laundry piled on the floor in the middle of the living room. What was she supposed to do? Her four-year-old mind was unsure, but her small hand wrapped around the big brass doorknob, turned it slowly, and then pushed open her bedroom door.

She found herself outside looking over the fence into her neighbor's yard. Lance plucked a squirming worm from the ground and cocked his head. "Heidi, come here. I have something to show you."

Heidi remained frozen on her porch and stood stoic, like

she'd just awakened from a bad dream. "I can't," she replied. "I think my mommy is dead."

Lance stopped digging and looked up at Heidi. Her words made no sense to him, but he could tell they were important to her. Several seconds passed before he stood and walked toward her. Heidi still didn't move. Her small round face's bewildered look prompted Lance to run into his house and fetch his mother.

Only later would neighbors wonder if they'd heard something strange or unusual. After all, their windows had been open, and their homes were relatively close to one another. But until later that morning, no one would understand the depth of the terrible violence that had occurred in the small house on a quiet street. The safe haven of Price would forever be marked by a homicide.

CHAPTER 2

LIFE AND LOSS

Me, Myself and I
Me, nobody really knows.
They know me by name but not
really what me is or what I am.
Me is a person that only a few people know.
I don't let everyone meet me but I'll let them meet I.

*Excerpt from a poem written by Loretta Marie Jones,
dated September 28, 1963*

Despite our differences in culture, religion, ethnicity, or social status, every human being shares one inevitable fate: death. It is a truth that no one can escape, no matter how hard we try to postpone or deny it. From the moment we are born, we are immediately given a place in that long (or short) line inching toward our destined expiration date; our time on Earth is limited. But while death is universal, how we die is unique to each individual. At best, we can hope to die peacefully in our sleep, but Loretta Jones, however, left this earth in the worst possible way: at the hands of another person.

Being stabbed to death is undoubtedly one of the most horrific ways a human can die. It involves the intentional and unlawful taking of a life, often accompanied by violence, fear, and trauma for both the victim and their loved ones. The act leaves deep emotional scars on those who survive and has a lasting impact on communities and society, as was the case for Price, Utah.

Loretta Jones. An unwed mother who stood strong above the bottom-feeding gossip and remained kind when others judged her. A mother who worked hard to provide for herself and her child yet continued to search for her soulmate, not out of necessity but to be honored and cherished til death do us part. This is the story of Heidi, the four-year-old daughter, who discovered her mother's body before she even understood the concept of death. It's also about a murderer who escaped justice for nearly half a century before the victim's daughter decided enough was enough.

Before we explore how a daughter fought for her mother's justice, let's rewind into the past and meet the mother who gave her life. Only then can we completely understand the full breadth of this story and the power of mother/daughter love.

Born in Price, Utah, on September 14, 1946, Loretta blossomed among her blended family. In a time when divorce was frowned upon, Loretta grew up in what some would consider an untraditional household.

LuDeen's second husband, Parley, originally from Elmo, Utah, had been married twice before and had three kids—

Duane, Glenna, and Verona—from his marriage to his first wife, Venola. His marriage to his second wife, Utahna, gave him his daughter Marilyn. With his third wife, LuDeen, they raised six children—Linda, Loretta, Conrad, Carolyn, Lila, and Bryon—and brought them up in the Church of Jesus Christ of Latter-day Saints.

The Mormon Church, officially known as the Church of Jesus Christ of Latter-day Saints, was founded in 1830 by Joseph Smith Jr. in New York. Mormons believe in Jesus Christ as their Savior, follow teachings from both the Bible and the Book of Mormon, and emphasize family unity and eternal relationships. They believe in modern prophets and ongoing revelation, with a focus on living according to moral principles and participating in sacred ordinances performed in temples.

The presence of the Church of Jesus Christ of Latter-day Saints (LDS) in Price in the seventies was significant. The LDS Church played a substantial role in the history and development of Utah and its communities.

Loretta grew up on 335 North 500 West in Price, in a modest house with a quaint front yard built by Parley in 1944. She attended Central Harding Elementary School, Price Junior High, and Carbon High.

"I remember growing up as kids, we were outside all the time," recalled Carolyn, Loretta's younger sister. "We were expected to check in with Mom while Dad worked. But he would come home for lunch each day." LuDeen and Parley were pretty open parents who didn't put too much pressure on their kids but did tell them once they learned to drive "not to pick up people on the road." Even though Carolyn recalled returning home from her grandma's house in Ephraim, Utah, and encountering two boys who had hit a deer on the side of the road. They were squeezed into the already packed car and instructed to sit on top of each other to give the boys a ride. According to Carolyn, Parley always did stuff like that to help others. However, she noted that, on the flip side, he was extremely protective of his girls. After Loretta's murder, his concern for their safety, as well as Heidi's, intensified.

Carolyn, who shared a bedroom with Loretta for many years, remembered Loretta in high school as having "a lot of different boyfriends" and said she teased her when a couple of boys from Spring Glen came over to visit Loretta by hiding behind the sofa and writing down everything they said.

Like many teen girls in the sixties and even today, Loretta kept a diary. Her first diary was a red-and-beige harlequin-diamond five-year diary with a lock and key. The pages were spaced into five one-inch sections, where she'd fill in the date at the top and write the year on the side. It was not nearly enough space for a hormonal teen to write all her feelings and fears, but Loretta's cursive entries filled every inch of space.

Her life recordings began on January 1, 1961, when she was fourteen. She wrote about her classes at school, gossiped about her girlfriends, and described outings and events with her tight-knit family. Woven between recounting her day-to-day life, Loretta penned a collection of hopes and dreams and, most notably, her loves and heartbreaks.

As was expected of a girl just discovering the butterflies of first love, the pages of Loretta's diary were filled to the brim with entries about boys. Over five years, she wrote again and again about one boy who seemed to hold her heart: Curtis S*[1]. He came and went throughout the pages, as did Todd*, Mark*,

---

1 In order to maintain the privacy of some individuals, their names have been changed, as noted with an asterisk*.

Carl*, and Ronnie*. But her love for Curtis stayed strong until finally, in 1965, they called it quits for good. She wrote: "Curtis and I broke up. I'm glad."

Many family members and friends described Loretta as "boy crazy." They recounted how she'd often fall into gloomy moods while waiting for letters and phone calls that never came. And if the calls did come, they were never from the boys she liked. In one sentence, she'd write them off for good; in the next, she'd be pledging her dying love for them. It was a pattern in Loretta's life, an important one that would come back to haunt her.

In 1964, Loretta graduated from Carbon High School. Her other sisters had dared to venture outside the small rural town of Price, so she followed suit and chose to attend the LDS Business College in Salt Lake City.

The LDS Business College was a private two-year college founded in 1886. The school was operated by the LDS Church. The college offered associate degrees and certificates in various business-related fields, including accounting, business management, entrepreneurship, marketing, and medical coding.

The college offered students like Loretta an opportunity to pursue a faith-based education while giving them access to a vibrant urban environment that provided opportunities for internships and networking. The school came with moral standards, which included using clean language, attending church services regularly, abstaining from sexual relations outside of marriage, and not drinking alcoholic beverages or smoking. It gave young students what was, for many, the first taste of freedom, yet backed up with a safety net held up by members of the church.

Loretta lived with a roommate while her father, Parley, footed the bill. Although she had more freedom than she'd ever known, she also had a plan. Loretta would graduate with an accounting degree and then return home so she could work for her father's business, Parley D. Jones and Sons. Parley operated a thriving contractors' business, overseeing projects such as constructing a library, a post office in Helper and Price, the Price courthouse, and Guido's grocery store, where penny candy was sold by the handfuls, bubble-glass containers lined up on the counter. Parley built many redbrick homes, which became his signature trademark in the area.

Despite experiencing her first taste of adult life, Loretta, only eighteen and right out of high school, struggled with homesickness. Her family was her everything, and the bustling streets of Salt Lake proved more overwhelming than she had expected.

Loretta's diary bore witness to her recurring dilemma, noting that every time she journeyed back to Price, the irresistible pull of homesickness would surge within her, eventually becoming so overpowering that it led her to make the life-altering decision to quit college and return to the comforting embrace of her hometown.

Loretta returned home only six months after beginning her studies at the business school and undergoing surgery on her chin for a cyst.

Despite not completing her accounting degree while in SLC, she pursued and successfully graduated through correspondence courses. Then she began working for her father, "keeping her dad's books," as she described in her diary. This included tracking and balancing expenses and revenue for her dad's company and generating all the associated bank and financial statements. She did it manually, with pen and paper and a typewriter, since it wasn't until the 1980s that accounting software became widely available and popularized.

Although Loretta was raised on LDS principles, she carried a rebellious spirit that set her apart. The church had strict rules on dating, kissing, and sex outside of marriage. They encouraged members to date other members with the same high moral standards and double date whenever possible. On May 15, 1965, Loretta wrote in her diary, "Met a guy. He said his name was Roger Draymond*. I guess I'll never see him again." But the following day, her entry read, "Went with Roger D. He gave me his [illegible] out of his car. I kinda like him. We drove around."

During that same summer in 1965, Loretta described herself as very tired. She started missing work. Her entries said she was worried and didn't know what to do. "Sick in the morning. I don't know what I'm going to do. I'm worried a lot."

July 11: "Dear Diary, Stayed home all day. I don't know what's the matter with me. I bet I'm PG. I don't know what to do."

August 19: "Mom asked when my last period was. I didn't answer her. I guess I should have. Oh well, I'm going to get a doctor's appointment."

On August 30, her diary entry confirmed that she was pregnant. It also stated that she wrote a letter to Roger D. After patiently waiting a week, Roger finally called, only to reveal that he was married and had been having an affair with Loretta, who was only eighteen.

"I don't know what I'll do now," her diary read. "I'm more confused than ever. Help."

Loretta confided in her parents that she believed Roger to be the father. The thought of navigating single motherhood in a small, judgmental town surely weighed heavily on her, evoking feelings of anxiety and fear as she contemplated her future.

"When you go from the living room, you could close that door in the hallway, and there was a telephone," Carolyn shared. "I remember going through the door and my dad being on the phone with a guy and upset about Loretta being pregnant. And I was trying to figure out what this all meant." Back then, these things within the family were kept quiet, and the children were never told Loretta was pregnant.

Lila was quite naive at that time. She recalled a moment from her school days when she mentioned, "My sister had a baby." In response, a girl asked, "Who was the father?" Lila innocently replied, "She doesn't have a dad." The girl gave her a funny look, but Lila was too young to grasp the underlying meaning of the question. Lila recalled that this was a hard time for Loretta emotionally. All she really wanted was a "good guy for her little girl."

Small-town gossip spread faster than wildfire and burned ten times hotter. Loretta was single and pregnant, a big no-no for the church and certainly frowned upon in society. The situation became unbearable for Parley, who was a highly respected and successful business owner who couldn't afford to have his reputation tarnished.

Parley took Roger to court, which embarrassed Loretta terribly, perhaps partly due to an undated note discovered in the back of her diary: "Blood test said Roger D. not the father."

On October 14, Loretta's diary read: "Dear Diary, Stayed home. I guess I should give my baby up. It would make it easier on daddy [Parley] . . . But I can't."

Carolyn mentioned that her parents supported Loretta, telling her that it would be her decision if she wanted to keep the baby. She emphasized, "But there was not a time that Loretta did not want to keep her baby."

October 27: "Mrs. Q. called me." [Mother of Mark Q*, whom she was currently "in love with."] "A girl has started a rumor at the high school that MQ [Mark] and I are going to have a baby. I wish it were true, but it isn't. She told me about it. I felt kinda stupid."

Loretta's diary also revealed that she was a faithful pen pal with many of the local boys who were serving in the Vietnam War. Almost every diary entry for 1965 mentioned Loretta writing a letter to a soldier, receiving a letter in return, or wishing to hear back from one of them.

October 26: "Got a letter from Stan*. He's going to Vietnam. I don't really like it." Many of her "loves" were servicemen, and she would wait eagerly for them to return home for the holidays or to visit their parents in hopes of seeing them. She'd write how some of these pen pals would never come home again.

After learning she was pregnant, Loretta mentioned many times that she would like a father for her baby and penned her dreams of finally being married, which might have been one of the motivations behind her correspondence with numerous boys serving in the war. However, Loretta never married, and Heidi Lynn Jones was born on February 14, 1966.

Motherhood came naturally to Loretta, and Heidi was welcomed into the big Jones family with open arms and open hearts. She had been the first grandchild born to Parley and LuDeen and was an easy baby to care for. It was expected that Loretta would take some time off to bond with her baby, and when she returned to work, LuDeen would watch Heidi while Loretta worked downstairs in her parents' home, keeping books for her father's business. Her single-motherhood status qualified her for welfare, which provided her with baby necessities as well as health care. Her job enabled her to make payments on a 1962 Chevy.

Heidi fondly recalled riding in the turquoise car, careful not to spill ice cream on the pristine white interior. Loretta often took her young daughter along while cruising around town with friends. With the radio playing and the windows rolled down, they enjoyed the freedom of no seat belts. Heidi's favorite flavor was vanilla, and she liked getting a cone from Sherald's Burger Bar, where they topped off the white swirl with a plastic animal figurine.

Photos captured Heidi, her blonde hair framing her brown eyes, being presented with a cake baked by Loretta each year to celebrate her birthday. In another photo, the cute four-year-old is smiling in a pretty blue-and-white dress that Loretta likely purchased at the local JCPenney store. The family album is full of these kinds of images.

Typically, children begin to retain memories of significant events in their lives around the age of four. At this young age, it's challenging to distinguish between actual memories and those formed from looking at photos, and Heidi was no exception. Nevertheless, all of Heidi's recollections of her mother were filled with positivity, wholesomeness, and warmth. Suddenly, all prospects for creating new memories with her mother were abruptly ended by murder.

CHAPTER 3

IMPACT OF A DEATH

It wasn't unusual for Parley to receive phone calls from the sheriff's office, as he did remodeling jobs for them and had just finished building the new courthouse. But after many persistent calls on this peaceful July day in 1970, LuDeen could tell by the officer's tone that this was not a business call. When Parley came home for lunch, Carolyn, Lila, Linda Lloyd, and LuDeen were all gathered around the kitchen nook. Parley's expression was somber and pallid. The sheriff's office had reached him at work. The weight of grim tidings was evident, and a heavy silence settled. "Did the sheriff's office not tell you that someone killed Loretta last night?" he said painfully. The room filled with collective despair as each of the family members tried to process the horrible news that Loretta was dead.

Upon processing the fact of Loretta's demise, LuDeen, seeking clarity, inquired about the circumstances. When Parley shared the devastating detail that she had been fatally stabbed and her throat slit, LuDeen's composure shattered, and she "lost it" and was overwhelmed by grief and shock. The kids sat in disbelief. Bryon was out bird hunting, so Carolyn's friend Linda Lloyd was sent to find him. The day remained a blur for Carolyn, and she often wondered how different each family member's perception of that pivotal moment would be if they ever sat down to discuss it.

Lila's recollection of that day was similar to Carolyn's, and Bryon confirmed that he had been out bird hunting with his BB gun but came in once found by Linda and was apprised of the horrible news.

Following the initial shock and denial, the Jones family experienced a roller coaster of emotions, leading to shifts in family dynamics as they adjusted to their new reality. After Loretta's death, the Jones family grappled with the raw and unrelenting pain of a void that could never be filled. And instead of talking about it, many members withdrew and emotionally detached themselves. Loretta's murder became a taboo subject. Any mention of it triggered an outpouring of tears from LuDeen.

Loretta's older half brother, Duane, shared that he and Parley were in the process of unloading a truck across from Loretta's house on the night of the murder. Bryon was there riding his bike, and they all observed lights in Loretta's house around nine p.m., but the lights had been switched off by the time they finished unloading. Despite initially intending to drop in and greet Loretta while he was in town, Duane refrained from doing so once the lights went out. This decision weighed on Duane as one of those hindsight moments.

Linda, who was very close to Loretta, was married and living in Idaho. The death of her sister was very painful and not something she felt comfortable discussing. Conrad was in the Navy and stationed in Hawaii but was flown back when he was given the news. Many years after the police had granted the Joneses access to the house, Conrad was given the horrible task of going in to clean up. He was the one who packed up most of Loretta's clothes and got the house ready for his new family to move in. It must have been traumatic for him to enter the house after his sister's murder and clean up her blood and the yellow chalk off the cold, brittle linoleum. Carolyn (seventeen), Lila (thirteen), and Bryon (ten) still lived at home. And then, after Loretta was gone, naturally, Heidi moved in with her grandparents, taking her new place as the youngest daughter and little sister.

Carolyn took advantage of therapy while going through some rough times in her life and found it helpful. "I don't feel my siblings have had anything to help them through. It would be helpful, even now, if we could get together and talk about Loretta. Everyone was hurting. Mom couldn't. Dad couldn't. That generation didn't talk through things much. When I left home and returned on weekends, I knew they loved me, but I never heard the words until much later, when I would say it first."

Carolyn shared that she heard Loretta tell their mom that somebody kept calling her. LuDeen encouraged her to report it to the police, but Carolyn didn't think Loretta ever did, and no records support that.

Lila fondly reminisced about her upbringing in Price, holding on to a "blind faith" that her family would always be all right. She always felt an inherent sense of safety and security in that tight-knit community. Until the day at the kitchen table when she heard the word *murder*. Then her whole world "flipped," and she never felt safe again. While the immediate worry centered on Heidi, Lila mentioned a disturbing rumor that suggested whoever had killed Loretta allegedly had photographs of all the Jones children, which could potentially put them in danger. Although just a tale, the fear it instilled in Lila was very real.

Lila's bedroom was downstairs, and from that night on, she would lie awake most nights listening to her parents as they paced above on the worn and creaky floor. This went on until Parley passed away when Lila was seventeen.

Playing night games as a child was a special memory of Lila's. Even though she was ten years younger than Loretta, she always felt special when her big sister would take her to hide. They would hold hands, duck into a dark spot, and wait to be found. "She was always so sweet and tender with me," Lila recalled.

When Heidi came into the world, the family's joy was palpable. Welcoming a baby girl was a special blessing, and her Valentine's Day arrival only added to her charm and sweetness. She was adorable, and the family was in love.

Lila became Heidi's primary babysitter, probably earning the going rate of fifty cents an hour in the seventies. Lila would watch Heidi when Loretta was working part-time at the Harding School library and when she went out on dates. Loretta taught Lila to make French toast for Heidi when she babysat, which was Heidi's favorite.

"Things like this don't happen in our town—first an attempted kidnapping and then a murder—and when these two things happen the same night, it sends people into locking their doors at night," the youngest son, Bryon, stated. It wasn't until he was past his seventeenth birthday that he stopped looking over his shoulder in fear of the killer coming back to hurt him or his family.

Sticks and stones can break your bones, but words can never hurt me. Carolyn and Lila learned the hard way that this childhood taunt was so untrue. There wasn't a place in this small town safe enough for the news of Loretta's murder not to reach and hurt the Jones family.

Carolyn overheard a couple of her high school classmates talking: "She deserved it." Carolyn went up to the two girls and said, "You don't know what you are talking about."

And they snottily retorted, "How do you know, Carolyn?"

Before turning and leaving the two chin-waggers with their mouths hanging open, she replied, "She just happened to be my sister."

Lila recalled shopping with Carolyn in the old Woolworths store, and a girl asked them if they had heard about "the murder" and then laughed in their faces when they told the girl that it was their sister. There were many times the murder was brought up in Lila's classes, and it would make her feel sick. So much so that attending school became hard for her.

Dying of a "broken heart" may sound like it comes from the pages of a fiction book, but it is possible. You might associate the breakdown with mental health, but it can take its toll physically as well. This is known as "broken heart syndrome." It is brought on by stressful circumstances, like the death of a loved one, cardiologist Tim Martin, MD, points out in a UnityPoint Health article.

Perhaps it was being the patriarch and trying to hold together a construction company, a young family, and a devastated wife that sent Parley to an early grave in May of 1974 at the age of sixty-five from a heart attack. His concern toward Heidi's safety was paramount, and Loretta's murder weighed heavily on him. "Dad was a prominent and cherished figure in Carbon County," Lila said, "and he was heartbroken that Loretta's case had not been solved. He never wanted the wrong person to be punished, but he wanted someone to be held accountable."

The weight of the murder was already a heavy burden, but when coupled with funeral costs, legal proceedings to adopt Heidi, and financial challenges that came from not being able to rent out Loretta's home, it intensified the strain on Parley. Bryon reflected, "All my dad's brothers lived well into their eighties. I'm convinced the immense stress hastened Dad's death."

When Carolyn was asked why the family still couldn't talk about Loretta's murder, she responded, "I think it was such a brutal thing that happened, and it has caused stress between us. However, things are getting better." They all agreed that it was just how that generation dealt with things. They didn't.

Lila said the murder was not discussed within the family to protect Heidi. They knew nothing of PTSD (post-traumatic stress disorder) back in those days, and the topic was just too painful for LuDeen. She and Carolyn had a handful of intimate talks, but for the most part, the weight and pain of the matter were concealed deep within their hearts, a private anguish they each bore.

After his father's passing, Bryon felt an immediate and pro-found sense of responsibility toward his mother. The words "take care of your mom" echoed incessantly in his mind, a poignant reminder of his father's last departure from their home. This deep-seated duty was what kept Bryon from leaving Carbon County.

CHAPTER 4

UNRAVELING A MYSTERY

In the hushed dawn of the quiet town, a young paperboy, his freckled face illuminated by the soft glow of the street-light, navigated the sleepy routes on his trusty bicycle. The spokes hummed a gentle melody with each pedal, blending with the sound of tires on pavement. With practiced precision, he expertly tossed rolled-up newspapers onto the porches of subscribers. Most of the time, the papers would hit their mark, while other times, they would land amid dew-kissed flower beds or just shy of the fence. He had read the headlines and felt responsible for being the bearer of bad news. The tragedy would find its way to the breakfast table to be digested alongside a cup of steaming coffee.

The *Sun Advocate*, a newspaper known as the voice of Utah's Carbon County, ran twice weekly in 1970. The paper detailing Loretta's murder was delivered on August 6, 1970, between five and six a.m. However, Loretta had died a week earlier, on Friday, July 31, and in a small town where everyone knows everyone, the newspaper was not the medium in which this tragic news had already spread throughout the community.

But the paper's article cemented what people believed they knew. And if anyone still hoped that the story wasn't true, the headline put that thought to rest: "Young Price Mother Stabbed to Death, Police Checking All Leads." The sizable black-and-white photo depicted Carbon County Sheriff Albert Passic and Price City Chief of Police Art Poloni bent over, examining the crime scene.

A photo in the bottom corner of the front page showed the modest one-story square house where Loretta and Heidi lived. Printed beneath it were the words: "Murder victim found here." It gave Loretta's home address and said the police had kept it locked since finding her body the previous Friday shortly before noon.

The article described the stabbing death of the twenty-three-year-old woman as a "bizarre crime." It stated that officers were continuing their investigation and searching for tangible clues that they hoped would lead them to the culprit.

The editorial went on to say that Loretta's body was found by her young daughter, Heidi, but incorrectly gave her age as three. She was actually four years old. It described how Heidi went outside, stood on her porch, and saw the boy next door digging up worms for a fishing trip. He called her to come over, but she replied, "I can't. I think my mommy is dead." Not fully grasping what Heidi was saying, the boy peered inside the house, spotted the bloody crime scene, and rushed home to tell his mother. Upon discovering Loretta's body, the boy's mother, Sue Ann Horvath, called the police.

The two law enforcement agencies working on the investigation said the woman had been stabbed and was found lying in a pool of dried blood. The murder weapon, what they suspected was a knife, had not been found.

Loretta's obituary also appeared in the August 6 edition of the *Sun Advocate*, along with a lovely black-and-white photo of the twenty-three-year-old single mother. "Victim of a murderous assault."

The obituary had already been published in the *Salt Lake Tribune* on August 2, only two days after her murder. It appeared on page fifty of the ninety-page Sunday edition under Intermountain Obituaries. Loretta was among twenty-nine obituaries, six of which included photos of the deceased, but hers had no photo. Only typed black words that bluntly listed the cause of Loretta's death as "Died from knife wounds." Next to her obituary was a notice for an unrelated family reunion, followed by a list of marriage licenses and births—death among life.

Also featured in the Sunday edition of the *Salt Lake Tribune* that day was an article titled "Police Press Probe in Price Death." The report included more details and the accurate age of Loretta's daughter, Heidi. It described the living room as "blood splattered" and said they had found the victim's body between the couch and a small coffee table.

It reported she had twenty stab wounds: two in the chest, seventeen in the back, and one in the throat. When her body was found, she wore only a blouse and brassiere. The autopsy performed Saturday was inconclusive insofar as determining sexual assault.

The news that day also mentioned the attempted abduction of a ten-year-old girl in the neighborhood that same evening.

According to the *Sun Advocate* article: Coincidentally, on the evening of the murder, police received a report that a man had accosted a ten-year-old girl on the sidewalk around the block

on Fourth East. Her apartment was a short distance from Loretta's home. She managed to escape and then gave the police
a detailed description. A search for the man that evening failed
to turn up any suspects. But the following day, after the murder
was discovered, an all-points bulletin was broadcast describing
the would-be molester, the theory being that the assailant and
the murderer might be one and the same person.

The girl, later identified as Lori Kulow, gave a report about
the incident, roughly transcribed below:

*I remember the night in July of 1970 vividly. I had been riding
my bike around the apartments while my brother, Jim Kulow Jr. and
Danny Malone were playing ball in the backyard. As I came around
the back of the apartment, I noticed they had gone inside, and it was
getting dark. I decided to go in as well, dropping my bike by the
kitchen window where my mom was doing the dishes. That's when
I saw a man walking; he had on a white T-shirt and blue jeans. I
thought he was coming to visit my mom's boyfriend, and it looked
like he was going to go down the stairs. Suddenly, he grabbed me
and pushed me against the building, put his foot on my feet, and
held my arms behind my back with one hand over my mouth. His
nails dug into my skin, making me bleed, and I knew he was a white
male. I tried to scream, but his hand was too tight. It only loosened
up when he felt a piece of gum in my mouth. I screamed loudly, and
he took off running. His hat fell off, and I thought he was coming
back for me, but he picked it up and ran away again. I then ran into
the house yelling, "That man, that man." My mom, brother, Danny,
and Jimmy Koffard all took off after him. I then yelled for my mom to
come back, and she called the police. Some neighbors outside said the
man ran down the street (south) and between the next two houses.
My brother and Danny had seen this man walking down the street
just before they went into the apartment.*

The next morning, I remember the sirens and police cars flying south down the street (going to Loretta's murder); it was like every cop in town went by. My brother had his baseball all-star game, and it was Saturday morning. My aunt Sharon picked me up to go to the south park. As I walked around, I kept thinking I was going to see the man or he was going to get me. My aunt had to run home for something, and I was worried about my mom, so I asked if we could stop and check on her. When we got to the house, the door was wide open, her purse was on the table, but she was gone. I started crying and thought that the man had come back and got her. I was so freaked out. We went back to the ballpark, and my mom was there in a police car looking for me. The police had come to the house looking for me because of Ms. Jones's murder and thought that the same man who killed her also grabbed me. They had picked up a hitchhiker in the Provo area, and they needed me to go and identify him. So my mom and I went with [Officer]Bob Tilton and another police officer to look at this man. They had found a bloody knife on him. But it definitely was not him; this man was too short and skinny.

Several days after this, Jimmy, Danny, and I went to the jail in Price to identify another man they picked up for the murder of Loretta Jones and grabbing me. It was hard to look through the screens, and I said, "I don't know if it's him." The thing I remember most was his hat; it looked like a bucket hat with different colors. I remember after I moved to Grantsville, Bob Tilton drove there to bring me a hat to identify. I didn't think it was him. The police told us (my mom and me) that they had to let him go after being in jail for three months because they didn't have enough evidence for the murder.

A man in Provo, a town about seventy-five miles northwest of Price, who matched the young girl's description, was apprehended and later released after he proved to have a valid alibi and could account for his whereabouts for the time in question. However, she was unable to positively identify their other suspect.

An anonymous phone call led police to a thirty-year-old Helper man, unnamed in the news article, who admitted knowing Loretta and being in Price that night in the area near her house and where the ten-year-old girl was accosted. However, after a period of questioning, the suspect requested an attorney, and investigators stopped questioning him. He refused to submit to a lie detector test and was released.

A follow-up *Salt Lake Tribune* article on August 3, headlined "Knife Probe Continuing," stated that officers had no new information. It reported that they had checked the victim's home for fingerprints, but the house appeared to have been thoroughly cleaned, and none were found. The report didn't specify who cleaned the house or how it was cleaned.

On August 8, a commentary on the case appeared in the Ogden *Standard-Examiner*, located 128 miles north of Price. It reported that Sheriff Passic had confirmed that the same thirty-year-old suspect was picked up in his home in Helper that Monday. He was driven to Price for questioning but was later released.

Since very little helpful evidence was found at the crime scene, the Price police investigators relied on the findings of the medical examiner's office. So, what was the result of the autopsy, and what did the medical examiner conclude?

The Office of the Medical Examiner (ME) employs a team of medical examiners, forensic pathologists, toxicologists, and other forensic specialists who work together to investigate deaths and conduct autopsies. They are responsible for determining the cause and manner of death for people who die suddenly, unexpectedly, or under suspicious circumstances.

This includes deaths that may be related to criminal activity, accidents, suicide, or any other events that are deemed questionable or unusual, like murder. The office often partners with law enforcement agencies, prosecutors, and other organizations involved in the criminal justice system.

Once the medical examiner assumes custody of a deceased body, they have the authority to conduct an autopsy, collect and analyze physical evidence, and perform toxicology tests, among other investigative measures. The medical examiner's findings and conclusions are then used to determine the cause and manner of death, which can be critical in criminal investigations, insurance claims, and other legal proceedings.

Medical examiner Edward F. Wilson, MD, performed the postmortem examination on Loretta Jones on August 1, 1970, at ten thirty a.m. She was case number 578-70. Wilson wrote his report using a manual typewriter, the standard of the time, written on State of Utah Division of Health, Office of the Medical Examiner letterhead. The seven-page report included Loretta's name, age, height, weight, and address.

The date and hour of her death were listed as 7-31-70 at 12:30 a.m. Beneath the "Circumstance of Injury" column, he typed, "stabbed by an unknown assailant," and he listed the cause of death as incised stab wounds of the lungs and pulmonary artery. The manner of death? Homicide. Under "Pathologic Diagnoses," there were two entries:

I. Multiple incised wounds with perforation of pulmonary artery, lungs, and heart, resulting in bilateral hemothorax.

II. Manual strangulation.

The general evaluation noted that the body was clad in a short-sleeve V-neck pullover and an unsnapped brassiere. Both were pulled up above the level of the breasts. Dried blood covered the pullover. The bra had a horizontal incision in the left cup, and the front of the pullover showed two incisions. Still, the majority of the stabbings were on her back, seventeen exactly.

As is usual in these cases, the ME collected swabs of evidence from her mouth, vagina, and rectum. Hair samples were logged. A piece of gray material found on the left side of Loretta's abdomen was collected and saved. Two Band-Aids were taken from the tip of her right index finger, covering a wound beneath her fingernail. She was wearing a green nonmetallic band on one of her left fingers and a school ring on her right ring finger.

On page six, under the "Respiratory System" column, Dr. Wilson listed a thyroid-cartilage fracture and hemorrhaging on both sides of the neck. In other words, although Loretta had been stabbed, manual strangulation had actually led to her death.

He also noted no evidence of injury to the internal or external female genitalia; however, another report found in Loretta's file stated: "Vaginal swabs (2): sperm present. Oral and rectal swabs: no sperm present." Blood tests were negative for alcohol.

Sheriff Passic commented that the autopsy findings by the medical examiner indicated that Loretta Jones had been sexually assaulted.

Now came the next step . . . discovering the person responsible.

CHAPTER 5

RUMORS AND GOSSIP

M ost of us have played the gossip game—where you whisper a phrase or saying to the person next to you. Then that person whispers what they heard to the next person, and the pattern is repeated as the message makes its way around the room. The fun part is when you compare the original saying with the message that the last person actually heard. The discrepancies are both humorous and alarming, especially when you think about directives that might really matter. But when the gossip is about a murder, the facts must be correct.

As with most small towns, plenty of rumors were going around about Loretta and the murder. People often projected their opinions, which turned into truths, and the further the information rippled, the more people felt they knew the facts.

Because Loretta was a single mother, it was often said that she was promiscuous. Remember, this was the 1970s, and it was still not widely accepted to be an unwed mother. Because Loretta dated "a lot" (define *a lot*), a popular rumor circulated, saying she was a high-priced call girl who entertained prominent community men whose names she kept in a little black book. These names included a mayor, police officers, prominent businessmen, and even someone connected to the mob.

Loretta had kept a diary; in fact, she had two five-year diaries: one that started in 1961 and the second in 1966. The earlier one has been accounted for and kept with Heidi's precious memories of her mother. The second one was supposedly taken by law enforcement to aid them in the investigation. If the latter one were anything like Loretta's writing style for the first five years, she would have included details of the men she was seeing and her likes and dislikes of them. It most likely would have also memorialized milestones in Heidi's life as well.

Had Loretta written the killer's name in this second diary, the one they called her "little black book"? What was the relationship? Was this why the diary was missing?

Before Heidi was born, Loretta's first diary listed several men she had been dating. She also speculated as to who the father of her unborn child was. One of the earliest rumors among those at the beginning of the case was started when Loretta learned that Roger Draymond* was not Heidi's father. Roger's mother was a nurse working at the hospital, and supposedly, she took and switched the blood tests so that her son would not be named the father. Blood-type tests later proved that he was not. Parley took the case to court, and as with any small town, it was probably a big embarrassment to Roger and his family. The news of this legal encounter probably spread like wildfire. The man was married, and it was probable that the affair did not sit well with his wife.

Would a man or his wife (or his mother) in this predicament have reason enough to stop the young mother from pursuing the relationship?

And what about the legitimate father? After Roger was out of the picture, had Loretta revealed the news to someone she thought to be the father, which caused him to silence her? In the 1970s, paternity testing for children wasn't commonly practiced. As a result, when Parley and LuDeen legally adopted Heidi, her birth certificate was altered to reflect Parley as her father. Despite the unusual nature of this arrangement, it was a legitimate adoption, and therefore, the document accurately recorded it as such.

What about a zealous suitor who'd learned she was carrying someone else's child? Jealousy is always a strong motive.

Perhaps Loretta had dated a few police officers or prominent businessmen. Was their reputation worth a murder charge? Even today, some believe the original investigation was a police cover-up to keep high-up individuals from being named in a scandal.

Heidi was four years old, so it didn't make sense that her paternity would be a volatile issue at that point, but perhaps someone had wanted to step in and assume the father role and Loretta was not keen on it.

So what about Bob? Who was this guy, and why wasn't he mentioned as a suspect? Was he even interviewed?

According to Carolyn, she; Lila; their niece, Cindy; and a friend, Linda Lloyd, were going to Moab the night of Loretta's murder and asked Loretta if she wanted to go. Loretta didn't want to bother her mother by asking her to watch Heidi, so she said no. Besides, she was waiting for her boyfriend, Bob, to visit her that weekend. Carolyn said she had even heard that Loretta and Bob were getting engaged but found it odd that no one in the family besides Lila had met him. Through the years, she would hear different stories about Bob: who he was, where he lived, and what he did for a living; however, Carolyn stated that Loretta personally told her that she was going to wait for Bob to come instead of going to Moab with them. "His last name might have been Blackwell," Carolyn reported. "It's hard to sort out what is real sometimes. Facts get twisted with time."

So was this Bob real?

Lila confirmed that there was indeed a Bob. He would drive Lila home after babysitting for Loretta when they would go out.

Bob was a truck driver by profession. Lila remembered how Bob showed Heidi a playful trick: teaching her to gesture like she was pulling an imaginary string to mimic the sound of a truck's air horn. Whenever Bob passed by their home, Heidi would perform this gesture, and in response, Bob would sound his horn, creating a cheerful exchange between them. Bob was never introduced to any of the family except Lila. She never learned his last name and thought he lived in Wellington, a town six miles from Price. "He was slim-built and very nice, and I can recall the car he drove but not how he and my sister met," Lila stated. The couple went out quite a few times, and Lila witnessed that they appeared to really like each other. "They laughed a lot," and he was indeed in Loretta's life for a short time, but the idea that they were getting engaged was never confirmed.

Lila was told that there was a young man sitting alone in the back of the church who was crying really hard during Loretta's funeral. Could it have been Bob? Would the killer put himself amid a family event and mourn the loss of Loretta?

Yes. This is actually a very common practice and has been for a very long time. One of the things that research has shown, fairly definitively, is that many murderers love to watch the effects of what they have done. So they attend wakes, funerals, and burials. They join search parties, put up flyers, and volunteer to assist the family or law enforcement. One criminal profiler goes so far as to say that 50 percent of the time, the murderer actually attends their victim's funeral.

In a statement made by Chief Poloni, a married man named Richardson was alleged to have been seen leaving Loretta's house the night of the murder, but no follow-up was mentioned.

And what about the pink roses that were left on Loretta's grave? No one had a clue as to who left the beautiful gift. Much later in the case, law enforcement was provided with Loretta's funeral book to review the list of attendees and perhaps identify a possible suspect. The giver of the pink roses was never identified, nor was anyone from the book interviewed as a suspect.

A Provo man was briefly apprehended for the kidnapping attempt on Lori Kulow, but he produced an airtight alibi. A Helper man was later jailed for the incident, but no formal charges were brought. This man was also a suspect in the murder of Loretta but was released after a preliminary hearing. He also had produced an alibi.

Is it possible that Loretta had seen something in relation to the kidnapping and she was being silenced? After all, she lived just a few blocks from the apartments where Lori Kulow had been accosted.

What about a total stranger? Could the bright lights shining through the windows of Loretta's home late at night have lured him in to rape the young mother, and the situation went from bad to worse? A burglary gone wrong? Were all these options explored? And who turned the lights out?

Experts argue that six motives explain homicide. Anger, concealment, jealousy, revenge, love, and gain. Certain personality disorders are associated with homicide, most notably narcissistic, antisocial, and histrionic personality disorders and those associated with psychopathology.

Stabbings reflect high physicality and unchecked emotion. Plunging a blade into flesh requires proximity and exertion, unlike the detachment of firing a gun. It's a very intimate act. Back then, law enforcement may not have been trained to recognize "overkill," where the number of stabs exceeds what's necessary to kill the victim, indicating a deep emotional conflict between perpetrator and victim.

Loretta did not seem like the kind of woman who made enemies easily. She was a hardworking single mother, just trying to live her life and raise her daughter. She was also a human being who wanted love and security and sought out companions to share her life.

She did not deserve murder.

CHAPTER 6

CASE NEWS

Rudy SanFelice, a local businessman in the seventies, owned the Newhouse Hotel on the corner of Ivy and Main Street in Helper. The beautiful old building is currently being restored; however, for many years, a weathered and burnt-out neon sign clung desolately to the side of the building's crumbling brick wall, serving as the sole relic of its former glory days. Built in 1912, the impressive hotel occupied the second floor, where most of its rooms were let out to railroad workers. A drugstore occupied the first floor. Stairs along the side led down to a cafe. And like many buildings around the hotel, they would soon vacate, leaving nothing but peeling wallpaper and cracked windows looking into empty space.

Rudy remembers when Tom Egley arrived in Helper. He was looking for a place to stay and seeking odd jobs around town to get by. All prior police records list Tom's previous occupation as a laborer. SanFelice rented him a room at the hotel and gave him a job pulling weeds and painting local buildings. Although Tom had multiple job opportunities around town, SanFelice recalls that he never seemed to get much work done. He would stay in his room most of the time, sleep all day, and then leave at night, often not returning until the morning. Rudy would later describe a strange vibe about Tom and pegged him as "sneaky." Tom seemed to get a thrill out of scaring people and would often creep up behind SanFelice and purposely startle him, and then, laughing, would say, "Did I scare you?" Maybe typical horseplay among friends, but SanFelice never considered Tom as such.

SanFelice's aunt and mother managed the Highway Rendezvous, a bar on Spring Glen Road. One night, Egley stumbled into the bar, out of breath, covered in what looked like blood on his arms, face, and on his white T-shirt. When people asked if he was all right, he said no and disappeared into the bathroom. His hands and face were clean when he emerged, but his clothes were still stained. The bar's owner, Margaret Hamilton, asked Egley, "What is that red stuff all over you?" To which Tom replied, "I'm painting for Barbara."

Barbara Battison (previously Barbara Busio), the owner of the Sportsman Club and another of Egley's employers, later insisted that she had given Egley very few painting jobs, none of which involved red paint.

At the time of Loretta's homicide, Tom was dating a woman named Marsha, who lived in Fountain, Colorado.

Egley had convinced Marsha to move to Helper in late 1969 or early 1970. When she arrived, she learned that Tom was living in a small hotel, getting by cleaning coal cars during the day and working at a local pub, the Sportsman Club, at night. Marsha was seven months pregnant with Tom's child, and SanFelice had noticed that Tom and Marsha were fighting more often near the time of Loretta's death. He noted Tom was acting strangely.

After Loretta's homicide, police questioned Marsha multiple times. They told her that Egley and Loretta had been dating before Marsha arrived in Helper. The police informed Marsha that the person who committed this crime most likely knew Loretta because there was no sign of a break-in and the fact that she was stabbed.

According to the Bureau of Justice, stabbing deaths are historically committed by someone known to the victim, usually a spouse, partner, or family member. Stabbing is also often associated with crimes of passion due to the up-close and personal nature of the act, which requires physical proximity to the victim and usually involves multiple stabs, suggesting a high level of emotional intensity. Additionally, the use of a knife as a weapon can be seen as an extension of the perpetrator's body, increasing the level of intimacy and violence in the act.

Investigators also explained that no money was missing from Loretta's purse and nothing was stolen from the house. Police told Marsha that Loretta's four-year-old daughter, Heidi, had been home at the time of the murder. When the police informed her that Loretta's autopsy findings discovered hamburger meat in Loretta's stomach contents, Marsha confessed that she knew about Loretta. Although Tom insisted they were just friends, Marsha said that Tom told her he had taken Loretta and Heidi to get hamburgers on the night in question. The fact that Egley continued to see the woman had been a point of contention in her relationship with Tom.

Chief of Police Art Poloni and Sheriff Albert Passic jointly headed the investigation. Eventually, they redirected their attention to local acquaintances of Loretta Jones. An anonymous phone call led police to thirty-year-old Tom Egley. Upon being questioned on August 3, Egley admitted knowing Loretta Jones and to being in Price on the night of the murder and confessed that he had been in the area when ten-year-old Lori had nearly been abducted. Tom refused to submit to a polygraph test and requested a lawyer. Further attempts by the police to interview him the next day were rebuked. Although (according to news articles) four other unnamed individuals were questioned, everyone had alibis for the date and time of the murder.

Sheriff Passic stated the findings during the autopsy indicated Loretta Jones had also been sexually assaulted. The attending physician on scene placed her time of death between eleven p.m. and one a.m. Tom denied any involvement in the murder and even stated he had an alibi.

After several items of physical evidence from the crime were sent to the FBI for analysis, the police felt they had enough to press charges.

The news of an arrest in Loretta's case brought immense relief and a renewed sense of hope to her family and the community. The weight of unanswered questions and the burden of grief began to lift, replaced by a glimmer of justice and the prospect of holding the perpetrator accountable for their actions.

The arrest instilled trust in the justice system and sent a clear message that violent crimes wouldn't go unpunished. The town could sleep again.

Sun Advocate, September 3, 1970:
Tom Egley was arrested and charged with the murder of Loretta Jones. According to police, Tom had been a suspect since the beginning of the investigation. He had been questioned twice during the investigation but, upon advice from legal counsel, refused to divulge information other than that he knew the victim and had visited her

home. Tom was declared indigent and was provided Attorney Thorit Hatch as his defense counsel. Hatch had been conferring with Tom since being questioned by police first. After police had received the lab report from the FBI, they felt they had probable cause to arrest Tom.

Tom was arraigned on August 31, 1970, and remanded to the custody of the sheriff's office to be held without bail. A preliminary hearing was set on October 8, 1970, but continued until November 5, 1970; the reason for the continuance was that witnesses had just been located, reports from the FBI lab had not yet been received, and Chief Poloni was in a school in New York City and was unavailable to testify. Defense Attorney Hatch argued that his client be released until the state was prepared to try the case. This was denied, and Tom was kept in custody without bail.

In a letter from 7th Circuit Court Clerk Michael Shane to Heidi Jones on October 12, 1989, Shane stated that the case files were no longer available, as they only kept them for eight years. However, he enclosed entries in the court minutes made by the court clerk in 1970. The entries were as follows:

November 5, 1970. The State of Utah vs. Tom Egley. Defendant, Criminal No. 6882. This was the day and hour set for the Preliminary Hearing of the Defendant upon the charge of murder. The defendant was brought before the Court and was represented by his Court-appointed counsel, Thorit Hatch. Dan C. Keller, County Attorney, and Boyd Bunnell, District Court Attorney, appeared as Attorneys for the State. Gayle Campbell, Court Reporter, was duly sworn by the Court to act as Court Reporter in this case. Upon motion of the County Attorney, the Court ordered all witnesses except Albert Passic, Carbon

County Sheriff, excluded from the Courtroom until called to testify. It was stipulated between counsel that the Defendant was present and reading of the Complaint was waived and copy acknowledged by Defense counsel. Sworn and testifying for the State were Sue Ann Horvath, Price, Utah; Parley G. [D] Jones, Price, Utah; Arthur Paloni [Poloni], Chief of Police, Price, Utah; Albert Passic, Sheriff of Carbon County, Price, Utah; Edward I. Wilson, MD, Salt Lake City, Utah; Charles Nelson Kirkwood, Helper, Utah; and Margaret Hamilton, Helper, Utah. It was stipulated between counsel as to the testimony of the FBI Lab, should they have been called to testify as to the results received in the report received from the FBI, Washington, DC.

State's Exhibits 1, 2, 3, 4, and 5, photographs of the deceased; State's Exhibit 6 was a plastic bag containing a pair of pink shorts and a pair of panties; Exhibit 7 was a plastic bag containing a small rug; Exhibit 8 was a plastic bag containing a pair of Levi's and a shirt; and Exhibit 9 was a signed statement from witness Charles Kirkwood. All of the State's Exhibits were offered and received in evidence, and the State rested its case.

Statements were made to the court by respective counsel, and the case was submitted. The court took the matter under advisement to rule at a later date, and the respective parties were to be notified.

Because Egley had entered a plea of not guilty to the murder charges, the court held a preliminary hearing to determine if there was enough evidence to proceed. If the judge concluded there was probable cause to believe the defendant committed the crime, a trial would be scheduled. However, if the judge did not believe the evidence established probable cause that the defendant committed the offense, the charges would be dismissed.

The state felt confident that from the circumstantial evidence, the lab analysis, and the witness statements, there was enough to hold Tom Egley over for trial. The family was hopeful and believed the state's arguments were solid. They only had to wait two days before the judge released his ruling.

From the Ogden *Standard-Examiner*, published on Saturday, November 7, 1970:

Utahn Freed; No Evidence

PRICE, Utah (AP)

Tom Egley, 30, of Helper, Utah, was released and a murder charge was dismissed Friday by Price City Judge, Tom G. Platis. Platis ruled early Friday afternoon there was not enough evidence to bind Egley over to District Court on the murder charge. Egley was charged in the July 30 stabbing death of Loretta Jones, 24, at her home in Price. Platis conducted a preliminary hearing for Egley Thursday, but postponed his decision until Friday.

From the *Sun Advocate*, published on November 12, 1970:

Tom Egley was released from jail following the preliminary hearing held on November 5, 1970. Judge Platis ruled the state had not presented sufficient evidence to hold him for trial on this charge.

The family stared in disbelief at the front-page photo of Tom Egley, head bowed, cigarette in hand, being escorted from jail by Price City Chief of Police Art Poloni. After three months in custody, he was now a free man.

It was a setback for the family that reopened wounds, plunging them back into the painful reality of their loss. They felt betrayed by the justice system and disillusioned with the notion of closure. Moreover, the uncertainty of not knowing who was responsible for their daughter's death left them vulnerable and helpless in the face of the unresolved tragedy.

Years later, during an interview, Judge Platis, who presided over Tom Egley's preliminary hearing, would vividly recall the case, as it marked his first experience with a murder trial.

Yet despite overwhelming circumstantial evidence, Platis could not proceed with the indictment. He confirmed that the only evidence the prosecution brought before him were the fibers linking Tom to Loretta's house. Even though these fibers had proved Tom's presence inside Loretta's home, they did not mean he had been there the night of the murder or was the murderer.

Tom's employer, Barbara, later said that Tom had told her that the police had found fibers on his clothes, which matched those found in Loretta Jones's house. Tom insisted they couldn't prove anything because he had been to the house before and had played on the floor with Loretta's daughter, Heidi. It only proved that he knew the woman, not that he had murdered her, and Judge Platis seemed to agree.

On November 6, 1970, Tom Egley walked out of court a free man, setting law enforcement back in motion to solve the case. They would need to explore new suspects and scenarios.

CHAPTER 7

FRAGMENTED CHILDHOOD

Sixteen-year-old Heidi Jones stood up in Mr. Scott's Creative Writing class, a wrinkled piece of paper in hand. No one liked reading aloud in Mr. Scott's class, but it was a huge part of the grade, and if students expected to pass, they had no choice. Mr. Scott explained that public speaking was a skill the kids would use later in life, and although Heidi didn't really buy it, she decided to take the assignment more seriously than others. For the last two nights, she stayed up writing and re-writing the poem until she felt she had it right. This was a hard assignment for her.

Heidi stood and moved shyly to the front of the class, passing her friends' desks and pausing beside the blackboard, where she waited for Mr. Scott to give her the nod to begin. The class had been studying Shakespeare's specific rhyming scheme, and the assignment was to write a fourteen-line sonnet. Although Heidi's poem didn't follow the parameters strictly, it packed a punch louder than any other poem read out loud that day.

Heidi's voice left her momentarily, and she stood alone in

front of her peers, whose judgment might hurt more than the words she'd written on the worn paper she held in shaking hands. All eyes were on her. *Don't cry. Don't cry.*

When she initially began to tackle this assignment, fear gripped her, stopping her from writing the first line. Her pen hovered over the blank page, uncertain where to start. How does one tell a story buried so deep it needs an earthquake to shake it loose? And should it be brought up at all? Why now? Yet once the ink began to flow, it bled onto the empty paper with fervor. And in the end, a peculiar emotion replaced fear, an emotion Heidi struggled to define. She believed it was hope, but hope alone felt insufficient.

Her poem was about a four-year-old girl named Heidi who discovered her mother's body in the living room of their house. It quickly became apparent that Heidi was describing her own experience, and a respectful hush filled the room. While adults like Mr. Scott had not forgotten about the unsolved murder of Loretta Jones, this was the moment many of Heidi's friends discovered why her grandparents had raised her and why it was hard to speak about her mother.

As an adult, Heidi still wasn't sure what led her to write this specific poem. Perhaps it was because talking about her mother's memory was taboo in her household and she had spent years trying to keep it bottled up. The few times Heidi spoke of her mother, her grandparents, specifically her grandmother LuDeen, couldn't handle it. Emotions became charged, and after some time, it was just easier to stay silent.

In many ways, Heidi's life had two parts: the one with her mother and the one without her. Like light striking glass and refracting on a wall, Heidi's memories of her mother's murder were fractured at best.

For her, reading a poem about a girl who found her mother's body was a way for her to describe an experience that didn't fully feel like her own. It was like watching a movie about her life and being told what happened to her.

Heidi's dissociation around this experience was the psychological defense mechanism that allowed her to disconnect from the emotional pain and distress of being involved in such a traumatic experience. Heidi's brain was attempting to protect her from pain related to the trauma by blocking or repressing memories. This can have a significant impact on a person's sense of self, as well as their ability to form healthy relationships and cope with stress.

At sixteen, Heidi had never been to therapy for what she'd experienced as a child. Although she had a support system and a safe home environment with her grandparents, she was discouraged from expressing any emotions about her mother. For Heidi, writing a poem about a child finding her mother's body was how she could process what had happened to her. Writing a story about her experience and its vulnerability was easier than confiding in her friends or attempting any further conversation with family.

Writing about a difficult event can help reduce the mental and physical burden of stress. It has been suggested that writing about trauma is like exposure therapy. Survivors also benefit from telling their stories because it helps them understand their reactions and manage them more effectively. Unknowingly, Heidi's writing assignment had been her first therapy session.

As the poem concluded, Heidi observed her voice, initially a whisper, now resonating with boldness and strength. A deep breath elevated her stature, and she raised her gaze to meet the eyes of her silent classmates. In their expressions, she found no judgment, only compassion, assuring her that everything would be all right.

The act of writing had liberated her. She realized her poem, first seeming to be the ending of a sad story, marked a new beginning.

Among Heidi's cherished childhood memories, one stood out vividly. She was standing in her yard, waving good night with her tiny hand at her grandfather, who was still hard at work outside his warehouse just a stone's throw away. Her grandparents, Parley and LuDeen, doted upon her, perhaps because she was their first grandchild and an adorable, sweet, loving little girl.

Parley had his successful construction business, and his wife, LuDeen, was a busy homemaker raising the last three of their five children at home. LuDeen had a green thumb and enjoyed growing hollyhocks, lilacs, and fruit on their property. Often, while Parley worked, LuDeen would take her children to visit the elderly and spend time with the neighbors. She was incredibly proud of her children and didn't hesitate to tell others about them.

Heidi was described as cute as a button. People in town always said, "You can always tell them Jones girls with their blonde hair and big brown eyes."

In the year 1973, when Heidi was seven, her life underwent a transformative shift as her grandparents went through the process of adopting her. Even though she was too young to grasp the legal intricacies of this significant change, she vividly remembered the precise instance her role shifted within the family dynamics. It was during a simple walk, hand in hand with her grandmother, when they encountered a friendly lady on the street. In that unforgettable moment, LuDeen proudly introduced Heidi to the passerby as her "youngest child," solidifying the new chapter in Heidi's life.

Heidi was unsure when she officially started calling Parley and LuDeen Father and Mother or when her aunt Lila, fourteen at the time, and her uncle Bryon, nine, became her sister and brother. It was hard for her to recall a time when this wasn't the norm.

Bryon felt that having Heidi come and live with the family was a pretty smooth transition. "I used to tease her all the time and would walk her to school and do all the things big brothers do. She just fit right in pretty easily and was our little sister."

LuDeen and Parley's history and connection to the church played an integral role in how they dealt with the aftermath of Loretta's murder. Although they didn't attend services regularly, they still considered themselves a part of the LDS community, and it was central to the way they lived their lives. In the 1940s and 1950s, the LDS Church generally had a conservative attitude toward therapy and mental health treatment. In some cases, church leaders at the time discouraged members from seeking therapy or professional help, instead emphasizing the importance of prayer, faith, and religious devotion to cope with personal challenges.

But in 1970, there was a much bigger stigma surrounding mental health than there is today. Childhood therapy wasn't important, and families felt certain issues should be kept private. LuDeen and Parley did their best with what they knew.

As a kindergartner at Price Elementary, Heidi was a quiet and shy student who had developed fears she couldn't entirely understand. When her aunt Lila, who was sixteen when Heidi was six, started dating her boyfriend, Rick, Heidi was cautious around him. She'd hide behind her grandfather's chair when he visited and appeared timid around all men.

In first grade, Heidi became friends with a girl named Becki, and together, they started walking to school every weekday. Occasionally, they'd see a man hanging around the schoolyard, and although he never spoke to them, Heidi was afraid of his presence enough that Bryon started accompanying them on their walks to school.

Despite everything, Heidi received good grades in school and appeared to be a well-adjusted child. Her introverted personality continued into middle school, as did her fear of men, something she couldn't quite articulate. It wasn't uncommon for her to cry to Parley, who sometimes just couldn't take it. He was a traditional man who believed in conventional discipline, and more than once, his frustration with Heidi would bubble up into a spanking as he'd repeat the old adage, "I'll give you something to cry about."

Among many cherished items from Heidi's past, she kept a two-page story she most likely wrote in fourth grade, back when cursive writing was practiced. One poignant memory captured in the recollection is of her and her mother ironing clothes together, side by side: Loretta pressing her work clothes while Heidi tended to her doll clothes—a heartwarming moment indeed. Loretta's talent extended beyond sewing her own clothes; she also crafted Heidi's attire and even fashioned the latest homemade styles for her dolls.

The story also reflected Heidi seeking safety in her mother's bed after a nightmare, and in the next sentence, she candidly expressed, "I don't remember anything neat about her [Loretta's] boyfriends. I don't even know who my father is."

Everything for Heidi changed in tenth grade, the year of the poem. She was sick of being a quiet and shy kid. She joined the volleyball team, expanded her group of friends, and boys started taking note of her. She'd cracked her own shell and developed a personality that became attractive to people her age. Her first date was with a local Price boy in ninth grade when he took her to the movies. She enjoyed mingling at the school dances and continued to get good grades. She stepped out of her comfort zone even more by joining the pep club and keeping stats for the school's team sports.

"I got a D- in home economics because my apron stitches were not straight." She laughed. "Maybe that is why I don't sew like my mother did." However, she picked up cross-stitching for a while but really got into crocheting after being taught by her sister, Carolyn, and made many lovely afghans.

For the most part, Heidi enjoyed school, but there was one class she and some friends would get in the habit of skipping. Seminary was a religious Utah education program for high school students, typically starting in ninth grade. The program included daily scripture study and discussion intended to help young LDS Church members deepen their understanding and commitment to their faith. She and her friends would "sluff" and enjoy drinking coffee at JB's with the cops who hung out there. Both skipping a religious class and drinking caffeinated beverages were Mormon no-nos. Heidi was rebelling.

This started happening more frequently when Heidi got her first car at seventeen, a maroon 1974 three-speed Camaro. She used the money from a savings bond her grandparents had bought for her. She also had a job at Golden Corral. Lila and Rick helped her pick out the car and pay for some small repair bills. It was a stick shift, and the journey home became her crash course in learning to drive one. Like most teenagers, Heidi liked to have fun and started hanging out at keg parties near the airport and drinking at friends' houses. Still, despite her having many close friends, she never opened up to them about her mother's death.

It was that day in Mr. Scott's class that, without realizing it, Heidi's life changed because she finally spoke out loud the secret she'd carried about her mother's death for all those years.

In order to write the poem and later read it, she had to fall into the abyss she had stepped over her whole life and try to recall the answer to the question that many people had asked her: What do you remember?

There were fragments of memories. A keyhole. A glimpse of her mother on the floor. Lance digging in the soil for worms and telling him that her mommy was dead.

And a name. One that stained her childhood and would follow her for half of her life. The name that became the reason she feared men as a child.

The name of the man who killed her mother.

CHAPTER 8

POWER OF THE PEN

C lad in cap and gown, Heidi joined her fellow 1984 classmates in celebrating their graduation from Carbon High
School. Together, they tossed their caps into the air, high
on the hopes of a bright future.

Heidi remained in Price until 1986, when she met Mike. She
was twenty, and he was five years older and played in a band
from Price. She'd party with the bandmates at bars and, in many
ways, became "part of the band." Heidi, too young to legally
drink in Utah but reveling in the moment, always had a good
time at the Hollow Bottle bar, thanks to the owner Terry Frye,
who made it a point to warn everyone whenever the police were
on their way. But then Mike moved to California, and she had
to make a choice. He was getting his own place and wanted her
to move there with him. It took her only a couple of months to
follow him west.

Heidi had numerous opportunities to break free from the
confines of Price. Alongside her sister Carolyn, friend Linda
Lloyd, and Linda's younger sister, Mary Ann, she embarked

on several road trip vacations. Their adventures included multiple visits to California, including the quintessential Disneyland excursion, as well as trips to the Oregon coast and Yellowstone National Park. In contemporary terms, these excursions would be deemed as "girls' trips." She would also spend an occasional summer in Salt Lake City. And although the prospect of leaving for new horizons filled her with an exhilarating mix of anticipation and trepidation, she felt she was ready to make her first significant step outside her comfort zone. It was with a resolute "yes" that she embraced the opportunity, for in her mind's eye, she painted vivid pictures of sun-soaked days and swaying palm trees. A welcome contrast from the dusty desert town of Price.

So, in July 1986, Mike flew back from California, and Heidi spent the night in Salt Lake City so she could pick him up from the airport. They would drive to California in her '78 Camaro, onto which her brother, Bryon, had welded a trailer hitch to the back so they could attach a U-Haul that would carry Heidi's belongings. Days before, she had mixed emotions as she packed up all her things and stood in the empty room of her grandmother's house, prepared to say goodbye to the only home she had fully known. She didn't want to think any farther back to her mother and the house where they'd lived before. Not when the sunshine of a bright future was streaming in through the window. Yet memories of her early life still existed in Price, the deep past blending into the present, staining the street corners, the shops, the schoolyard—and the police station where the cops investigated her mother's case.

In many ways, she felt she was leaving her mother behind. Guilt murmured inside her head not to leave, but her heart felt the embrace of her mother's arms, and she was whispering to

Heidi that it would be okay. She would always be with her. *Go. Live your life.*

One of the items Heidi took with her when she left was her mother's cedar chest. The beautiful piece of furniture had always been one that Heidi cherished. Since it was filled with Loretta's handmade items and keepsakes, Heidi had a tactile connection with her mother. LuDeen was not pleased with her taking the beloved item, but Heidi was no longer the child who had been told to keep silent about things other people didn't want to discuss. So, the day Heidi left Price, she asked her grandmother for the extra set of keys to her car and LuDeen asked for "her" house key back. A massive fight erupted between them. Still, Heidi took it because this was the one thing she had left to remember her mother, and she felt it was rightfully hers.

For the next seven and a half years, she and Mike enjoyed living in the Golden State. She quickly found employment at a travel agency but worked there for only two months before beginning a more stable career in the real estate industry. Certainly, she had the freedom to experience the life she'd always dreamed of, but the pieces just didn't always click into place, and the sunshine-and-beach lifestyle she'd imagined didn't unfold precisely as she had hoped. Sunshine sometimes burns too hot.

Heidi and Mike eventually split up, but before Heidi left, and with Mike's full support, she began writing letters about her past to various people involved in her mother's murder case. She was looking for a way to solve her mother's death. Again, writing became her therapy.

Heidi became an avid viewer of the popular documentary television series *Unsolved Mysteries*, which explores real-life unsolved cases, including murders, disappearances, and other mysterious events. Each episode typically features interviews with family members, witnesses, and experts, as well as dramatic reenactments of the events. The show originally aired from 1987 to 2010 and was later revived by Netflix in 2019. The program aims to bring attention to these unsolved cases and potentially generate new leads or tips to help solve them. What if Heidi wrote to them and they aired her mother's case? She wrote down the contact information listed at the end of a segment and promptly wrote a letter, sealed the envelope, slapped a stamp on it, and crossed her fingers.

The process got her thinking: What if she wrote letters to others who might also have information on her mom's case? Why not?

Most of the correspondence started out in the same manner: "I am writing to you in hopes that you will be able to provide me with some information regarding a murder case that happened back in 1970."

Heidi Jones was twenty-three when she wrote her first letter in 1989. As an adult living in the shadow of her mother's death, it had never occurred to her that she might play a part in the future solving her mother's cold case. She had long ago accepted that her mother had been killed and the murderer had gotten away with the crime. End of story . . . or so it seemed.

Little did Heidi know that the initial letter would ignite a compelling desire that propelled her into a continuous letter-writing journey. It was a pivotal moment that summarized her past and led to a different future. Since writing the poem in high school, it was perhaps the first time she had actively confronted what happened to her as a child and became a participant in her destiny. Much of her life before this had been an exploration of her self-identity, one she was still uncovering. Her mother's murder was no longer "something that just happened" but became a lingering question of "what if?" What if she could help solve this crime? What if she played a part in closing the doors on something that had not only ended her mother's life but had also grown to define her own in many ways?

Heidi's letter was not the first written on behalf of Loretta's case. Linda, Loretta's older sister, had written a letter to Dan Keller, Carbon County attorney, in 1971. The family was frustrated and wanted to know what was being done to find Loretta's killer. Mr. Keller's response was very interesting but left the family with little hope.

September 30, 1971
Dear Linda,

I received your letter of September 12 and give you the following information: Investigation is continuing with respect to the murder of Loretta. I must frankly say, however, that no additional or new leads have turned up. Following the dismissal of the case against Tom Egley, the officers started over again, searched through the house again, and have interviewed everybody that they would have any reason to interview and have given some polygraph [lie detector] examinations. Such has not produced anything, however, and it appears obvious that some lucky break will be needed to find the guilty party.

In all probability, there are people who know something they have not told and eventually this information may come out. That is about all we can hope for. The case certainly is not closed, however, and the officers will continue to follow up any leads that they get.

If you have further questions or if I can supply additional information please let me know.

Best wishes,
Dan
Carbon County Attorney

From 1989 to 1990, Heidi began a letter-writing crusade. She wrote fifteen-plus letters to the following people, sometimes more than once: Carbon County Court House Records Department, Dan Keller, Gene Strate (County Attorney 1989), 7th Circuit Court, Price City PD, Albert Passic, US Department of Justice, FBI, Ron Todd (AG in SLC), Utah Attorney General, Dean Holdaway, Vicki Salzetti (friend of Loretta's), and the television show *Unsolved Mysteries*. She received no response from the program or the Price City Police Department. All other replies either yielded no new information, indicated the absence of existing records, or suggested alternative avenues to explore, ultimately leading to dead ends.

Yet the murder of her mother followed her into adulthood and cast a shadow on her life. It had become a part of her, always hovering beside her, something she neither openly acknowledged nor tried to resolve. Growing up with her grandparents, she'd learned to accept that death was just a part of life and it was something better not to spend time thinking about. But now she was thinking about it. Very much. If so many cases were being solved on *Unsolved Mysteries*, why not her mother's?

Although she visited Utah about once a year, she found Price to be stuck in a bygone time warp, and it no longer felt like home. She saw her grandmother on every visit, but still, after all these years, the murder of her daughter was not something LuDeen was willing to talk about. For that matter, it was still a taboo subject for most of the family.

After leaving Mike and getting her own apartment in 1994, Heidi stayed in California for another ten years. She actively dated but never lived with anyone in California again. Her letter-writing campaign intensified, and she became relentless in her pursuit of justice and decided to return to Utah, where she moved in with Rick and Lila.

She also wanted to confront what she'd experienced as a child and unload the weight she was carrying. While in California, Heidi had seen three different therapists. The first was a waste of time, the second was "okay," and the third, who used guided imagery techniques, showed promise, but the sessions concluded right when they were making progress. Her job had ended, thus suspending any therapy benefits. Back in Utah, she figured she'd give it one last try to unlock something in her memory. "I know I know more," she stated. She wanted to heal, and in that first hour's session, black mascara ran down Heidi's cheeks as she shared the memory of discovering her mother's murdered body when she was just four. It was hard to get the words out, and she felt exhausted from the emotional purging. She felt she had talked for hours, and at the end of the session, the therapist asked, "Why are you here?" *What?* The question shocked Heidi. It was not a response she expected; needless to say, she never returned.

Heidi also turned to an alternative avenue, seeking answers. Not necessarily to aid in unraveling the murder but to connect with the spirit of her mother. California was one of the states where world-renowned self-proclaimed psychic/medium John Edwards held his heavily attended events. Lulu Martinez, Heidi's friend, attended with her and sat in the packed arena with ten thousand others to hear the popular speaker. The air buzzed with energy as Edwards helped many reconnect to lost loved ones through his uncanny ability. Heidi hoped her mother would "come through," and just as if he read her mind, John Edwards belted through his microphone, "Oh, and somebody on this side of the room lost a mother at a young age." Lulu grabbed her friend's arm and said, "Heidi, Heidi!" but Heidi couldn't move or talk. A woman in another part of the crowd yelled, "That's for me," and Edwards said, "No, it's not you." Heidi explained that this type of "validation stealing" happens often at these events, as everyone is hopeful that their loved ones will "come through" for them.

Heidi had also given her friend Lulu a dozen blue roses for her birthday, so when the psychic Edwards told a story of blue roses, it solidified their belief that Loretta was connecting with them.

Lulu and her husband, Rick, attended another John Edwards event much later (2017). Heidi could not attend, but they reported back to her that her mother, Loretta, had also come through at this event. They sent her texts and a bracelet with a note she had written about what Loretta wanted Heidi to know. Through Edward's events, Heidi felt she had a connection with her mother, and that was what she needed.

All this was a comfort to Heidi. However, writing those letters became her catharsis, the outlet she didn't know she needed until she started doing it. She was on a mission to discover her mother's murderer, but finding the man responsible and getting a conviction was most likely impossible. No matter the circumstances, Heidi found solace in giving her feelings and thoughts a voice, releasing them from the depths of her heart and sharing them with the world. She understood there would be roadblocks along the way, but regardless, her unwavering determination propelled her to seek out information and forge a path through the detours that could potentially open up directions to resolve her mother's case.

By the time Heidi moved back to Utah in 2006, exactly twenty years after she'd first left, she was convinced the little four-year-old was correct in who she believed killed her mother and was now focused on the pursuit of him.

CHAPTER 9

MEMORY OF A MURDER

For Heidi, returning to Price was like leafing through the pages of a treasured book. Time had bestowed wrinkles upon some pages, blurring their once-vivid details, while others stood as crisp and legible as the day they were written. And although a few of the characters had changed or moved on, the overall story stayed the same.

Heidi, now a grown woman, five feet five with shoulder-length reddish-blonde hair, could confidently walk the streets and face her reflection in the storefront windows without being overpowered by the shadow behind her. Her essence, the one who had experienced trauma and learned to suppress it, still silently hovered nearby, separate from her but always a part of her identity.

Driving through the small town, she found herself parked in front of *the* house. Her house. Still standing on 468 East 400 South. It had belonged to her grandfather, but this was the first place she called home until she moved in with her grandparents. For a short time, Heidi and Loretta lived in an apartment across from a popular park on the other side of town and then in a house behind Loretta's cousin Maurice. Heidi vaguely recalls specific details of those homes, unlike the one where her mother died.

The structure was intact, and the yard was freshly mowed; it was different but somehow still the same. She sat and stared at the house for some time. It appeared to be weeping. So much so that Heidi longed to run to it and embrace it. It spoke to her in ways only Heidi understood. Comforting her as well as encouraging her to move on as it had, now occupied with new life. Renewed. Renovated. Upgraded. Do this for yourself, Heidi, it seemed to say. Move on with your life. Open the windows and let the light and fresh air in.

She thought about the boy next door, Lance Horvath, her playmate and first friend. She smiled at the memory of the two of them sharing secrets and toys through the fence that separated the two properties. The towering tree, which they had once imagined to be the home of an owl, stood steadfast, its leafy canopy still casting cool shadows over the idyllic playground that remained the perfect haven on sweltering summer days. Although abruptly broken, their connection would always remain in those carefree moments.

Memories that most children under four would probably forget, Heidi still remembered. Little details, like the doll her mom made her and the color of her toy box. The sewing machine that her mother used to sew and create many of Heidi's clothes was kept in the corner of the house. The beloved teddy bear and little things Loretta knitted.

The layout of the house had been basic. A small, comfortable front room furnished with a small couch and stereo. A string of blue, black, and green beads, decor popular in the sixties, hung across the doorway of Loretta's bedroom, establishing her private space. Those beads were still kept in a small box in Heidi's garage. Old bubble bath bottles filled with blue water sat neatly on shelves, and the house smelled clean except for days when Heidi's mom would bake cakes. On those days, sweet smells wafted from the oven, and Heidi remembered kneeling on a chair next to the table, watching her mom decorate the cakes with fun frosting and figurines. Occasionally, she would dip her little finger into the sweet, gooey batter, but Loretta didn't mind.

Always the mannered host, Loretta kept an ashtray in the house although she didn't smoke. Her nature was a collector and a crafter. Several books relating to the supernatural, astral readings, and powers of the cosmic universe were kept in an old magazine rack. The talking board game Ka-Bala—"the mysterious game that tells the future"—was kept in the closet along with a Ouija board and the Game of Life. Loretta frequently accompanied her mother to Mrs. Olive Nelson's house for fortune-telling and tarot card readings. *Dark Shadows* was one of her favorite daytime TV soap operas, and they enjoyed watching it together as well as dancing around the living room to Jan and Dean records.

Loretta's father, Parley, owned the house where Heidi and Loretta lived. Still, he didn't play favorites, and even though Loretta was their only unmarried child with a baby, she was expected to pay her own way. To do so, she worked for Parley, keeping his books and helping with his business. A job she enjoyed and was skilled at.

Heidi had no memory of being warned about "stranger danger" or being coached about people who might try to hurt her. Before the murder, all her thoughts were wholesome. Positive. Carefree.

In many ways, trauma had time-stamped her life, but details of what happened in their house existed in fractured pieces. Somewhere among those fragments was the truth.

That first memory of looking through the keyhole with silent confusion, knowing she was witnessing death's solemn presence but not able to comprehend its weighty significance, unsettled her.

Crossing Main Street, Heidi found herself meandering to the north side of town. Autumn had shaken the leaves, and they were piled high in yards for children to enjoy one last time before they were gathered up for the year. She pulled up in front of a church and turned off her engine, matching the silence of the town.

Loretta's funeral was held in the white-brick LDS Price Second Ward church pristinely situated on the hill up from the city park and was handled by Fausett's Mortuary. The church aisles overflowed with hundreds of people waiting to pay their respects to the slain young mother. Flowers were arranged artfully around the casket, and the scent of roses lingered in the air. Empty tissue boxes were quickly replaced as people sitting on wooden pews cried softly. A respectful hush was accompanied by faint organ music.

Mourners reverently bowed over the soft-brown mahogany casket that held the delicate body of Loretta Jones to pay their respects. The open lid was lined in light-blue and white satin. Soft and velvety to the touch. The casket stood too high for young Heidi to look into, but she recalled unfamiliar hands that tenderly lifted her, offering a brief, bittersweet glimpse of what she couldn't comprehend—this would be a last goodbye. Loretta, lying as if asleep and offering a peaceful smile, was dressed in a beautiful blue-and-white high-collared dress, the color matching the lining of her coffin. Heidi recollected that she looked like Sleeping Beauty.

There was one memory from that day that Heidi wasn't entirely sure was her own. A vision of Grandma LuDeen pulling down the collar of Loretta's dress to show Heidi the slash marks on her neck. Had she just heard about this? Or did she actually hold the memory of the knife wounds across her mother's neck being concealed by the high-collared dress chosen purposely by the family to hide the awful truth? It could be due to confabulation, a memory error that can occur during traumatic situations where an individual confuses a story as belonging to their memory or can often remember something that didn't actually happen. In retrospect, showing a young child her mother's slashed neck seems strange for a grandmother to do, and there was no reported "slashed throat" noted in the coroner's report. The medical examiner had labeled the cut on her throat as a "horizontal incised wound that measured 1 1/2 inches in length and 1/4 inch in width." However, Carolyn, Loretta's sister, relayed the same story, saying, "It was so weird and bizarre to this date." She described how her mother, LuDeen, would pull down Loretta's collar to show where her throat had been slit. "It had clear tape, like packing tape, over it. She would then put the collar back up and show the defense wounds and the bruising on her legs."

Yet amid the haze of uncertain recollections, there are other facts that Heidi had never once doubted. And those memories belonged to the source of the actual trauma—her mother's murder.

On the evening that Loretta died, Heidi vaguely recalled her mother putting her to bed, a familiar routine after a bedtime story. But that night, probably after a knock on the door, she believed her mother had told her to stay in her room no matter what she heard. Heidi still wasn't entirely sure if her mother knew something terrible would happen that night or if her mother was trying to get her to sleep. Nevertheless, regardless of age, some memories clung to the child, disregarding the passage of time and remaining etched in her consciousness with a tenacity that defied forgetting.

Heidi recalled one vivid and clear memory. She looked through the antique keyhole of her bedroom door. There had been no sound coming from other parts of the house. Just an eerie nothingness. But what sound does murder make? She remembered being very hesitant to leave the safety of her room the next morning and, according to the police report, waited until around eleven a.m. to venture out, still clad in her nightgown. She was fairly certain that she played with her toys until late into the morning and speculated she stayed in her room trying to be good and obey her mom's instructions. The silence was daunting, so eventually, Heidi believed she called out for her mom, and when she didn't get a response, she looked through that keyhole. The big brass doorknob was right above it, just one turn away from the front room. Through the small slit, a beam of light filtered in, verifying to Heidi that it was morning. That was when she saw "something." It looked like a pile of clothes on the floor. Taking tiny steps, she inched toward the mysterious bundle. Sunlight penetrated through the window, illuminating the room with dancing dust particles. Apart from this delicate display, the air felt stagnant, devoid of any life, as if time had come to a standstill.

Heidi quickly realized it was not a pile of clothes lying in the center of the room. It was her mother. Heidi was frightened by the amount of blood that seemed to be everywhere. She noticed her mom was still wearing the pedal pusher pants (a cross between pants and shorts) from the night before. They were pink.

Like a robot, Heidi walked outside and found herself on the front porch staring over the fence at her friend Lance Horvath. He asked her to come to his yard because he had something to show her.

Formulating the next few words must have been hard for the four-year-old. Not because she couldn't say them, but because she wasn't really sure of what they meant or if they were true.

"I can't; I think my mommy is dead."

As an adult, Heidi would lament the fact that this was her first experience with death and that she wasn't even sure how she knew her Mom was dead. And yet, for the longest time, Heidi associated all death with murder. They had become synonymous to her.

The next thing she remembered was sitting in the Horvath kitchen. Beyond that moment, her memory was a blank slate. However, a faint, persistent feeling from that day forward continually gnawed at her. She knew who the killer was, and now she felt compelled to piece together the evidence to prove that her memory from that fateful day was not a mere creation of a child's imagination—but she would need help.

CHAPTER 10

COLD CASE

new name to the College of Eastern Utah's staff roster was added in 2007. Dr. Rachel Walton, author of *Cold Case Homicides: Practical Investigate Techniques* and coauthor of *National Best Practices for Implementing and Sustaining a Cold Case Investigation Unit* as well as many journal articles. Dr. Walton was hired as a criminal justice/sociology professor. She is a thirty-two-year veteran of law enforcement and criminal investigation and widely regarded as an internationally recognized authority on practical cold case homicide investigations. Part of her experience included training law enforcement agencies on cold case homicides.

Her book and her reputation prompted Price City Police Chief Aleck Shilaos to contact her in early 2008. He phoned Dr. Walton and said he had heard she had been hired by the College of Eastern Utah. He wanted to have lunch and have her sign her book, *Cold Case Homicides: Practical Investigative Techniques*. He also wanted to talk to her about an unsolved homicide in his department. They met, and Shilaos handed her the remaining

Loretta Jones case documentation: four newspaper clippings. Chief Shilaos invited her to assist with the case, and like many past cold cases Walton had worked on, she started with limited information. She developed a five-page suggestive investigative plan, a to-do list to get things rolling, and the PD opened Cold Case #20080157 on February 4, 2008.

Again, they weren't surprised. Sheriffs are elected officials; if defeated, it wasn't unheard of for them to become bitter and take records home or destroy them. Occasionally, police departments merged with sheriff's offices and files were lost. Before the era of digital files became commonplace, relying on paper records posed the risk of them deteriorating or getting lost over time.

After compiling the data they received, Walton and Henrie determined their baseline number hovered around 208 un-solved murders in Utah between 1965 and 2005. The number might not seem high to some, but for Walton, it represented as many as 208 murderers still unconvicted, possibly roaming free. Some of these were likely multiple murders committed by the same individual.

Price City Police Officer Kevin Mele was assigned as the detective on the case. Together with Walton, they worked on gathering information from the medical examiner's office, the FBI lab, living witnesses, and other resources. They were able to locate the son of the late Sheriff Passic. He could not find any notes or files, but he said his dad often spoke about a case "where the guy was guilty as sin."

Sue Ann Horvath, the neighbor who found Loretta's dead body, struggled to recall details accurately, as her health was in decline, and her two boys, whom she had spoken to about the case in the past, had no fresh information to offer.

Walton and Mele returned to the 468 East 400 South crime scene and spoke with the family now renting the home.

They also looked into then-suspect Tom Egley, who had been arrested and released. Walton judged he would be in his late sixties, and they'd need to locate his date of birth and isolate the surname *Egley* out of many to one specifically connected to Helper, information that they eventually found.

Then there was the surviving family. Loretta's mother, Lu-Deen, was still alive, and there were many siblings. And what about her daughter, Heidi? One of the to-dos on Rachel's list was to locate her.

Officer Mele checked with County Attorney Dan Keller and Judge Platis for any case files. On February 28, 2008, he met with Madalene C. Williams, a secretary for the county attorney, who had been working there since 1979. Williams knew of the Loretta Jones case but said the office had no information. However, she mentioned that in 1989, there had been a request for information made by Heidi Jones, Loretta's daughter. Madalene had written a response indicating that no records before 1976 were retained by their office. She explained that by law, the county attorney does not have to keep permanent records except in felony cases that have been bound over to district court. This case was probably handled in the circuit court, where the court only had to keep records for seven years.

As it turned out, Williams knew the family. She had grown up next door to the Jones family and kept in touch with Heidi and Loretta's sisters, Lila and Carolyn. However, when asked for their contact information, Williams was hesitant, unsure how they would feel about the case being brought back to light all these years later. Still, she would do her best to get the contact information the PD needed. Small towns are protective of their friends and family, yet Madalene and another clerk meticulously searched through all the docket books and found no records. She signed off the letter to Heidi by saying, "I really wish I could be of more help."

Walton studied the case newspaper clippings from the 1970s. She wrote summaries and her thoughts about Loretta's murder and the local investigation surrounding Tom Egley.

On March 3, 2008, Walton joined Detective Mele to interview former Price Chief Arthur Poloni. Although Poloni was initially suspicious about their renewed interest in the case, he eventually opened up to them. The retired chief discussed his interviews with Thomas Egley and described how Egley said he knew Loretta Jones but hadn't seen her for a couple of days before her murder. In Egley's second interview, Egley broke down crying at one point. Poloni was convinced they were about to get a confession out of him, when another investigator interrupted them.

Still, Poloni didn't finger Egley as the man who'd killed Loretta Jones, instead saying he suspected a married man Loretta was rumored to be having an affair with. The man had been seen walking away from Loretta's home that afternoon or evening. When they questioned him, he had an unshakable alibi. Poloni could not give Mele a name or further details regarding this speculation.

According to Poloni, about three to four pieces of evidence had been sent to the FBI lab, including a T-shirt believed to be Tom's and a knife blade found near the railroad tracks behind Jones's house. Other than the statements from Tom's girlfriend and his clothing (with blood tests showing no results), they had no more evidence, which was the main reason the case was dropped at the preliminary hearing.

After the interview, Walton assisted Officer Mele in cowriting their report and gave it to Chief Shilaos.

Heidi was not even aware that Price City had an open case regarding her mother's murder. She learned this from Lance's brother, Eddie Horvath, and then she had to meet with the county attorney, Gene Strate, to find out what was happening.

Heidi found it difficult to comprehend why investigators were listing her whereabouts as unknown. In fact, Heidi took matters into her own hands by going to the police department herself and meeting with Chief Shilaos. During their conversation, Chief Shilaos remarked that they had been unaware of how to locate her. In response, Heidi pointed out, "My grandmother is still alive; all you had to do was ask her."

A document in the file, dated May 4, 2009, contained an email from Heidi to the police chief. This email relayed details about Heidi's conversation with her grandmother, LuDeen. In this communication, LuDeen expressed her deep distress over the fact that Tom Egley, an early suspect, had not been handcuffed or restrained during the hearing, allowing him unrestricted movement within the courtroom.

The next email had no date, but Heidi thanked Aleck (Chief Shilaos) for taking the time to meet with her and her family. She encouraged him to speak one-on-one with LuDeen, as she felt it might yield some information Heidi had been unable to get from her since she became very emotional when speaking about Loretta's death.

Heidi recalled meeting Chief Shilaos in his office in 2009, where he made the comment, "Too bad there are no photos of the crime scene." Heidi said she jumped up, left the office, and returned with four Polaroid photos.

The images were black and white, framed in the Polaroid

style, with a white border with extra space at the bottom to write a caption. Heidi remembered coming home for visits from California and she would be leafing through all the "happy happy joy joy" photos and then *boom*, there were these four awful photos of her mother's murder. She would skip through them and one time worked up the nerve to ask LuDeen, "Why do you even have these in here?" LuDeen removed them soon after, and when she needed them for Chief Shilaos, she had to grovel to get them back. Shilaos scanned them, and Heidi gave the originals back to LuDeen. Heidi had not seen them since.

Around August 2009, the case started to stall, and Walton hadn't heard much from Chief Shilaos. That was not to be unexpected, as her role was strictly as a consulting resource, not as an investigator. About six months later, she ran into Officer Mele and asked about the case. Officer Mele told her that once Chief Shilaos had discovered there was no DNA evidence connected to Loretta Jones's cold case, which the district attorney said they would need, he closed the case. Ultimately, Chief Shilaos decided to close the investigation, which Walton disagreed with, but it was out of her control.

While her involvement in Loretta Jones's cold case first started in 2008, when she wanted to research unsolved homicides across the state, so she and her coworker, retired law enforcement officer Scott Henrie, created a survey to send to each Utah law enforcement department. From experience, they knew cases overworked most police departments, and most officers didn't have time to answer lengthy questions. For that reason, their survey asked one single question: How many unsolved homicides did you have between 1965 and 2005?

It took some time to get the responses, which didn't surprise Walton. For decades, evidence rooms have been moved and files have been purged. The standard practice used to include trashing evidence after some time had passed. It would take the departments some time and research to answer even one question. Eventually, Walton heard back from all twenty-nine sheriff's offices in Utah and 66 percent of the police departments. Some gave answers; some said they didn't know.

Heidi had not heard about Price City closing the case and continued to contact Chief Shilaos with questions about its status.

From: Heidi Jones
Sent: Wednesday, September 02, 2009, 1:00 PM
To: Aleck Shilaos
Subject: Anything?

Hi there Aleck,

I just wanted to check in with you to see if anything from my mom's funeral book popped out at you. There were some names that my aunts questioned about—especially the guy that left the two pink roses. But it didn't ring a bell to me. Do you know if Gus Pappas is still alive? And if you have had a chance to talk to Boyd Bunnell—and have you had a chance to talk to Tom Egley?

I would be very interested in talking with Rachel Walton, too—I have left her a message, but I have not got a phone call back.

Hope all is well—
Thanks, Heidi

(Gus Pappas was a very prominent man in Carbon County whom Heidi felt might have some information, and Boyd Bunnell was the district attorney in 1970.)

> *From: Aleck Shilaos*
> *Date: Wed, Sep 2, 2009, 1:10 PM*
> *Subject: RE: Anything?*
> *To: Heidi Jones*
>
> *Boyd Bunnell indicates he does not remember or have anything concerning the case. Which really surprised me. Gus Pappas has passed. Walton has seemed to lost interest and have not heard or seen her in weeks . . .*
>
> *I do not think talking to Mr. Egley will accomplish anything . . . still thinking about that.*

Unbelievable was the word that came to Heidi's mind when she received that email back from Chief Shilaos. Heidi thought, *Perfect, we should turn the case over to the sheriff's office, then,* and on September 29, 2009, Heidi conveyed to Chief Shilaos her desire to transfer the cold case file regarding her mother's murder to the Carbon County Sheriff's Office. She expressed frustration with the limited efforts the police department was dedicating to her mother's case. There were moments when she sensed she was providing Shilaos with more information than he was actively investigating. Clearly, the case was not a priority for them and the statement that Walton had lost interest was not true.

It was not usual for cases to be transferred at the request of a victim's family. However, Chief Shilaos seemed to have no issues returning it to Carbon County, the original investigative agency in 1970. And it was there that a bygone acquaintance of

Heidi's now worked as a sergeant. As a result of her request, all the information the Price Police Department had collected was transferred to the Carbon County Sheriff's Office. That included the photos that Heidi had provided them from the murder scene, including one that contained some interesting evidence that Shilaos had missed.

CHAPTER 11

DAVID BREWER

In July 1970, at the time of the murder of Loretta Jones, David Russell Adams was six years old. The middle child of five, he and his siblings were living at Camp Pendleton, approximately thirty-eight miles from San Diego. Each morning, they would walk to school, which was situated just outside the base's main gate. It was a comfortable childhood, one he enjoyed. His father was in the Marine Corps; his mother was a housewife.

David didn't recall ever being told not to talk to strangers or being afraid of playing outside his home unsupervised. Even after the family moved from Southern California, he didn't recall fear as ever being a part of his younger years. His parents knew his friends and whereabouts but never smothered him. "Helicopter parents"—those who pay excessive attention to a child's every move and experience—were still a phenomenon far off in the future. He had a good childhood and dreamed someday of becoming a police officer.

But at fourteen, everything in David's life changed on the flip of a dime. His parents divorced, and his mom remarried another Marine, Mark Brewer, who would later adopt him, giving him the name David Brewer.

"That change had everything to do with the church," Brewer recalls. Mark was a member of the Latter-day Saints (LDS) Church and wanted to build a strong family unit centered on Mormon values.

David genuinely appreciated his new stepdad, Mark, for the most part. Their relationship flourished primarily due to Mark's grounded approach. Reflecting on his biological dad, David remarked, "My real father was more inclined to discipline us with a butt whooping, something we likely had coming."

Moving from Southern California to Salem, Utah, in 1978 was a big culture shock for David. Salem was a postage-stamp-sized town of 2,200 people, with one grocery store, one gas station, and not much to do. Spanish Fork, the nearest high school, became David's educational retreat during grades eight through ten, and he commuted twenty-two miles round-trip daily by bus.

He and his siblings were required to attend church, fast on Sundays, and complete four years of high school seminary. He has nothing negative to say about the LDS religion, but following their high school years, he and his siblings were no longer active members.

The summer before his junior year, David's mother informed him they were moving again, this time to Price, Utah, sixty-eight miles south, and it would be there that David and Heidi would first cross paths. Upon the family's initial arrival in Price, David fondly remembered his mother taking him on a scenic drive around the town, affording him the opportunity to "check it out" and get acquainted with their new surroundings. He was struck by the charm of a lovely park, and the West

Wood neighborhood where they bought their new house was much more appealing than their previous residence in Salem. However, his friends from his previous high school warned him that he would be in a fight before he graduated from Carbon High because that was "just the kind of place" he was moving to. And they were right.

Moving to Price granted his father the luxury of avoiding the long commute from Salem to his current job at Valley Camp Coal Mine. David settled into his new environment and liked his new school, Carbon High. Still feeling a bit like a transient, he fit in the best he could. Military brats understood that being considered an outsider was just part of life.

"If I can remember right, I have lived in forty-six houses in my lifetime," David recalls.

Art was his favorite subject, and he took Spanish in his junior year, winning an award from Brigham Young University for an essay he submitted. Team sports weren't his thing. LDS dances became David's preferred pathway for meeting girls, and shortly after graduating, he received life-altering news: he was going to be a father. He and a girl he had been dating welcomed a baby girl into the world, but they did not marry. Instead, he and another woman tied the knot when he turned nineteen.

In 1985, at the age of twenty-one, David woke up and decided he needed to find direction in his life. A little discipline, some structure, and a reliable paycheck would do him good. Following his father's and stepfather's footsteps, he called a Marine recruiter, and soon after, enlisted in the Marines Reserves, signing a six-year contract. The two-thousand-dollar enlistment bonus was a solid motivation. Still, the real inspiration came from the opportunity of a new career. Computers were fairly new in the mideighties, but David caught on to the technology and used his skills throughout his six-year stint. While fax machines seem archaic today, they were a new technology in the eighties, and David worked on the first ones on the market.

Being in the reserves, David triangled between Camp Pendleton in California, Overland Park in Kansas, and his home in Price, where he spent most of his time and could pursue other careers. In fact, for the first two years of his time in the reserves, David worked two jobs: McDonald's, a position he'd begun in high school, and Price Auto Parts. He moved on from those jobs in 1987 and labored underground, working on conveyor belts for three years in Carbondale, Colorado, at Mid-Continent Coal Mine. In 1990, an opportunity came his way when a friend who owned a Subway franchise asked him if he wanted to buy it. He couldn't escape the claustrophobic confines of the sooty black coal mine soon enough and jumped at the opportunity. He not only ran that Subway store for twelve years but, at one point, owned four franchises, including the Subway that replaced Price's iconic Arctic Circle. Little did he know that the long-forgotten restaurant would reenter his life in a consequential way after he had moved on from his days at the Subways.

Although he made good money with the Subway franchises, money wasn't everything. David began looking for a new career that would provide him with a sense of purpose. He had always sought more from life, driven by an innate desire to improve, excel, and leave a lasting impact. Yet the question lingered: What would be his next step?

He no longer wanted to just stay busy. He wanted to channel his energy into something of value. This drive to contribute something positive to society led to his decision to become a police officer. In 2002, David applied for a jail opening at the

Carbon County Sheriff's Office. Although he wanted to keep two of his Subway stores while he attended the police academy, his now-second wife at the time felt she couldn't manage them alone and stamped a big NO on the idea. So the stores were sold back to the friend who had initially brought him into the franchise. A win-win.

At thirty-eight years old, David finally reunited with his childhood dream to become a police officer. Growing up, he'd always envisioned wearing a badge proudly on his chest. He'd listen to police scanners, eagerly consuming any crime in his town, and never missed a TV episode of *Cops*. Not only did he grow up next door to one of the few female police officers on the force, but once, he witnessed a wild police chase ending in his front yard. Exhilarating moments like this stuck with him through childhood, into his career in the military, and later into his thirties.

Looking around at the young, eager recruits on his first day at the corrections academy, he surmised that he was probably the oldest student there. It turned out he was the second oldest. A female classmate, one of the lucky ones who had survived an abduction by the infamous serial killer Ted Bundy, decided to become a police officer following her horrifying experience. She was allowed some time in class to speak about her frightening encounter, providing David's class with a unique perspective from a survivor of a brutal crime.

Like all recruits, David was required to pass a physical test to graduate. While training in the Marines, such a test would have been a breeze. He stood five feet eight, with serious blue eyes framed by wire-rimmed glasses, and his brown hair sported the standard military crew cut. But after long hours spent managing a Subway shop and watching the Raiders play football on Sundays, he was no longer in peak physical shape. As a result, the running test remained his persistent Achilles' heel, a challenge he grappled with until the very last day, when he ultimately managed to pass but only by a narrow margin of ten seconds.

After graduating from the academy, David worked in the jail for his first two years as a sworn deputy. Monitoring inmates, searching for contraband, enforcing rules, and keeping order became his daily routine. He initially had no desire to leave the confines of his jail position. Gradually, the pressure from his peers won out, and he took the initiative to get back into shape and get out on the road. He reenrolled in POST (Police Officers Standard Training) for the law enforcement block, and this time, he excelled. At forty years old, he impressively completed the running requirement with a mile time of 10.04 minutes, securing the top spot. His hard work paid off, and after a few years, he was promoted to detective and later added a new stripe to his uniform when he became patrol sergeant. He gradually worked his way up the career ladder to day sergeant.

Becoming a cop seemed a logical next step for a man who valued justice and was eager to uphold the law. He stood taller and swelled with pride each time he stepped into the world wearing his uniform. Knowing that his actions could potentially prevent harm and protect others brought him a profound sense of purpose and fulfillment in a world filled with uncertainty and danger. Whether it was lending a helping hand to those in distress or actively working toward solutions to societal issues, he found solace in the belief that his efforts were making a tangible difference in creating a more secure and harmonious world for everyone.

Over the years, David divorced, remarried a third and fourth time, and had more children. Juggling the responsibilities of his role as a deputy with the delightful chaos of a household brimming with kids brought him immense satisfaction. He became a grandfather relatively young, and although he had twelve grandkids, he didn't get to see them as much as he would like. That was because, unlike traditional grandparents, David wasn't retired yet.

Seven years after becoming a sheriff deputy, David ran into a Carbon High classmate, Heidi Jones, at a local art festival. Although they had moved in different social circles in school, he vaguely recalled their shared classes and remembered glimpses of her at McDonald's, where he had worked as a teen.

This was not an accidental meeting on Heidi's part. On August 17, 2009, Heidi converged on David with an essential purpose: to look into the unsolved murder case of her mother, Loretta Jones.

CHAPTER 12

NEW SET OF EYES

T urning to the sophomore page of the 1982 Carbon High School yearbook, a captivating photo of a young Heidi Jones, her radiant smile lighting up the page among her fellow classmates, is displayed. A determined expression graces her face, her eyes gleaming with unwavering resolve. A subtle hint of a mischievous smile plays at the corners of her lips, revealing a spirited and resilient personality.

Toward the end of the yearbook, the image of David Brewer in a blue tuxedo is proudly showcased amid his senior class. His graduation class was only a couple hundred, so it was easy to know all the students, if only by sight. Therefore, although they didn't interact much in high school, Heidi and David knew of each other. Heidi's memory retained enough of him that his name remained imprinted in her mind a quarter century after graduation. Fate would lead her back to Price, where David, the same David Brewer she remembered, still called the city home. However, a significant change occurred when David Brewer became a detective for the Carbon County Sheriff's Office.

This new bit of trivia planted a seed in Heidi's brain, and it began to grow. What if Brewer's position as a detective could help solve her mother's murder? Her attempts to get the case resolved had been met with little interest. No one seemed to be listening.

It didn't matter that she and David weren't close in high school. It mattered to her now that he represented a connection to her past, a tether to the life she'd left behind, and a glimmer of hope for the future. She had an "in." What if Detective Brewer could offer a new set of eyes and was willing to help?

So she pursued him on Facebook while the question lingered. It finally took root and blossomed on July 24, 2009, when Heidi's car was stolen. She was living in Kearns, Utah, and had posted, "Oh no—my car's been stolen." Soon she received a reply from David that read, "Too bad you aren't closer." That's when Heidi learned that David was still living in Price. She read one of his posts informing her of his plans to attend the Helper Art Festival, so she made it a point to be there and hopefully run into him. She was on a mission. The festival was in full swing, and the closed-off streets of downtown Helper were blocked off to allow art vendors to sell their crafts in canopy-covered booths. Walking through the maze of people with a girlfriend, Brenda, Heidi spotted David pushing a stroller and walking with his wife. With confidence, she approached him, hit him on the shoulder, and said, "David freakin' Brewer!" His face showed no recognition. "I'm Heidi Jones, and I'd like to talk to you about a murder that happened in 1970."

David's response? It was very much a "here we go again" moment, but he was kind enough not to roll his eyes. This wasn't the first time someone had approached him asking him to look into a case. It was a by-product of wearing the badge. As a cop, people assumed he was always on duty, able—and willing—to help. Sometimes, the requests were simply for directions, and sometimes, like Heidi, they asked for much more.

Initially, David just blew off the request, almost as if she hadn't asked. He was trying to enjoy the festival's gaiety with his family, and a woman he barely knew from high school was asking about some old case from decades ago. He didn't have the time or patience to get involved. Their interaction was short, but David gave her an opening: "Here's my card. Give me a call sometime next week, and we can talk."

The weekend ended, and David had shrugged off the encounter, half expecting not to hear back from Heidi and half planning how he'd kindly turn her down if she did contact him. But bright and early Monday morning, his phone rang. Heidi was asking if they could meet in person. He agreed, still not expecting much. They met in his office, and Heidi pushed a folder across his desk containing paperwork and photos. She then sat back in her chair and recounted the case details. Thirty-nine years ago, her mother, Loretta Jones, had been murdered, and the case remained unsolved, her killer walking free. Would he help? Could he take a look at the cold case?

Brewer was now intrigued. As a detective, cold cases had always piqued his interest. He told Heidi he would consider it, not knowing that by agreeing to investigate Loretta's case, he would become Heidi's biggest supporter and Loretta's best hope at finding her killer beyond the grave. Heidi left ecstatic, and by the end of the day, all the files she had accumulated over the years were stacked on Brewer's desk.

After researching the details of the case, Detective Brewer discovered Loretta Jones's murder was an original case with the Carbon County Sheriff's Office. He asked Sheriff James Cordova if he could work the case, and with his support, he reopened the case and quietly worked it in the background among his other duties. And so began a seven-year journey that would eventually become one of the most demanding cases Sergeant Brewer had ever tackled, but it ignited an unyielding determination within him. Being a detective was his passion, and he eagerly embraced the challenge this cold case would give him.

By the time Heidi reconnected with Brewer, he had advanced from deputy to detective. There was a reason he was good at his job. He worked all his cases—from jaywalking to homicide—with the same level of importance. Brewer possessed an unbiased nature, giving him a clear, nonjudgmental perspective as he focused on any case, old or new. If a drug addict were robbed, Brewer wouldn't write him off, blaming them for putting themselves in that position. He was the kind of cop who looked beneath the surface and saw people for their humanity. He understood that a junkie could be a victim too.

From what he could tell at the outset of Loretta's case, he believed the original investigation in 1970 was poorly conducted, partially because of preexisting biases from the original deputies. Not only was Loretta Jones a single mother, something still frowned upon in 1970, but she also had a reputation for dating around, something other men looked down on at that time. Detective Brewer suspected the previous deputies may have carried prejudices when they approached the investigation and may not have taken it with the same care as someone who left their opinions at the door. There were no files or details to aid Detective Brewer in reopening the case. And after forty years, 90 percent of the witnesses were deceased. Brewer found the prospect of a more challenging case intriguing. After all, detectives thrive on solving puzzles.

Fortunately, Heidi had been gathering information independently since 1989 and had more in her possession than the sheriff's office had in evidence for this case. Detective Brewer carefully sifted through her twenty-year collection of detailed notes and documents. Some of her material included the letters she and her family had sent to individuals who'd worked on the original case, but the responses provided minimal help. Brewer knew he would need to dig deep to uncover the answers Heidi had been unable to find.

Cold cases—unsolved crimes that have been open for years, if not decades—often lack immediate leads, witnesses, or conclusive evidence, making the search for answers quite taxing. Brewer would first need to examine any original case files, review witness statements and forensic reports, and identify patterns or overlooked pieces of evidence. He would then need to locate and reinterview witnesses—if he could even track them down. Hopefully, he could take advantage of technological advancements to reexamine old evidence to find new clues that could lead to the identity of the perpetrator.

As noted in the file Detective Brewer received from the PD, a report from Dr. Walton was mentioned. Brewer reached out to Walton, stating he was familiar with her report to Chief Shilaos, and asked if he could get a copy. Walton agreed to help after getting confirmation to release the documents from the Price Police Department.

Brewer delved into the cold case, seeking answers. Walton became a key resource, aiding him with insights and brainstorming sessions, making them a formidable team on the case.

CHAPTER 13

Where To Begin?

F irst, Detective Brewer searched for the 1970 case file but
found none in the sheriff's office archives. The demolition
of the old building and the move to a new facility meant
that many files were lost, possibly discarded, or destroyed. Additionally, court records were elusive; neither the judge nor the
district court had any trace of the case. This was because the
charges against the suspect, Tom Egley, never advanced past
the preliminary hearing, leaving no official court records.

Next, Brewer contacted the state medical examiner's office
and was relieved to discover they had a report from 1970. The
autopsy showed that a vaginal swab had confirmed that Loretta
had been raped, since semen was present. The initial autopsy
report and evidence from the crime scene, including pieces of
DNA, were released to Deputy Ned McCourt with the Carbon
County Sheriff's Office on August 1, 1970. Thirty-nine years
later, Detective David Brewer received the same report. Now
he had to track down McCourt to find out what happened to
the evidence.

Ned McCourt vividly recalled the case but told Brewer that he had no memory of receiving the evidence from the medical examiner. If he had received it, the evidence would have been placed in the evidence room at the sheriff's office in Price. Even though Ned was an eighteen-year veteran deputy at the time of the murder, he said he had never seen such a brutal murder.

The cause of death was listed as incised stab wounds of the lungs and pulmonary artery. The pathologic diagnosis, which covers the cause of death and any contributing factors that could have potentially played a role, listed the following: 1. Multiple incised wounds with perforation of the pulmonary artery, lungs, and heart resulting in bilateral hemothorax. 2. Manual strangulation.

In plain English, the pulmonary arteries are blood vessels that carry oxygen-poor blood from the right side of your heart to your lungs. In Loretta's case, this artery, as well as the lungs and heart, had been perforated or cut multiple times, causing a consequence from the traumatic injuries. Manual strangulation, also known as throttling, is a type of asphyxial death where the perpetrator uses their hand to encircle and compress the front and side of the neck. It is a common method of homicide, most often encountered when the physical size and strength of the assailant exceeds that of the victim.

He recalled that the head investigators in the case were Price Chief Art Poloni and Carbon County Chief Deputy Albert Passic. Detective Brewer discovered that both investigators were deceased, Passic in 2007 and Poloni in 2008. However, Poloni, who had retired from the department in 1974, had been interviewed before his death about the case by the Price Police Department, who also interviewed Passic's son. Brewer learned the details from their report.

In the interview, Poloni recalled that at the time of the murder in 1970, the Price City Police Department had only four or five deputies, and the city had a population of four thousand residents (1970 US Census cites 6,718). He recalled Price as a relatively safe town, so much so that in twenty-five years on the force, he'd only drawn his weapon three times.

When asked about Loretta's murder, he recalled that someone called police headquarters to report that "an individual at 468 East 400 South was hurt and bleeding and crying." This is interesting because the reports later state that Loretta had been dead long enough for the blood to dry. Poloni was the first deputy on the scene. When he arrived at the address, neighbors stood in the street crying outside the single-story wood-frame residence. He asked what happened, and a girl whose name he didn't recall said, "Loretta is in the house." He found her lying in the living room to the left of the front door, and although it was clear she was dead, rigor mortis had not yet set in.

Poloni believed that Tom Egley was not the killer. He thought it was a married man with the last name "Richardson" (he couldn't recall his first name). And he remembered Richardson's wife was dating another man. Richardson lived in the upper part of town and had been seen walking away from Loretta's residence that afternoon or evening. However, Richardson's alibi was "unshakable."

When asked how Egley became a suspect, Poloni stated that Barbara Busio, who had hired Egley for temporary jobs, reported him. Egley's girlfriend, who lived with Egley at a local hotel, told Busio that Egley came home early, around three a.m., changed clothes, took a shower, and then took those clothes to a laundromat. He then came home and went back to bed.

Poloni added that a bartender at the Rainbow Inn (it was actually found to be the Highway Rendezvous) in Helper claimed that Egley came into the bar later that night with blood on his shirt. Poloni explained that Egley was interviewed twice. Egley was taken to the sheriff's office interrogation room after Busio reported him. When asked if he knew Loretta Jones, he confirmed he did but hadn't seen her for several days. Egley claimed he didn't own a knife, the suspected murder weapon. Yet he was known as an amateur whittler who carved wood. A knife blade was later found near the railroad tracks behind Loretta's house. But it was never connected to Egley.

During Egley's second interview with Poloni, he recalled that Egley broke down crying, and Poloni suspected he was close to confessing something. But another investigator entered the room, and Egley shut down and asked for an attorney. Egley was eventually arrested, but Poloni said the judge ruled they didn't have enough evidence to hold him. When asked what evidence they did have, Poloni noted that Tom's girlfriend was a witness, and they had his clothing. However, the clothes had been washed, and the blood tests used at the time couldn't find any evidence of DNA.

Detective Brewer was determined to build the case impartially. He didn't assume Egley was guilty and aimed to clear him of the crime if possible. Aware of the danger of prejudice clouding judgment, he resolved to base his conclusions strictly on facts, remaining unbiased throughout the investigation. Brewer was committed to following protocol and would adhere to "innocent until proven guilty."

At this point, Detective Brewer knew the next step he needed to take in the case. He wanted to interview the two women Poloni had mentioned: Egley's then-girlfriend, Marsha, and Barbara Busio, the informant who'd reported Egley's name to the police.

But before following those leads, he decided to meet with Loretta's mother first.

On August 20, 2009, Brewer visited LuDeen Jones for what would become the first of many visits. All these years later, LuDeen still recalled certain things surrounding the case and preliminary hearing. She told Brewer she remembered standing in the courthouse with Egley and saying to him, "I hope you rot in hell for what you did to my daughter." And then LuDeen repeated again how Egley replied, "You know I did it, and I know I did it, but you can't prove it." They all recalled that when Heidi came to live with them, she repeatedly said, "A tiger killed my mom," and, "Tom killed my mom." So much can be implanted into a young girl's mind, so Brewer took this with a grain of salt. He also knew how badly the family wished for someone to be held accountable for the murder of Loretta.

Both LuDeen and Loretta's sister Carolyn recall Tom's attitude in court as cocky. A woman named Margaret (Maggie) Hamilton (now deceased) testified she witnessed Egley with bloody clothes. However, a man named Charles Kirkwood, who was an acquaintance of Tom's, supplied him with an alibi that he was with Tom the night Loretta was murdered. The alibi was a strong point in Tom's favor, but unfortunately, Brewer couldn't verify it with Mr. Kirkwood because he was now deceased.

One of the people whom Brewer wanted to find and interview was Tom's then-girlfriend and now-ex-wife, Marsha. But all he had was her married name, and a search for Marsha Egley produced nothing. He knew that Tom and Marsha had a child before they were officially married, so, through records at the Utah Health Department, he was able to obtain her maiden name and where she was from. Continuing a name search, he contacted the Otero County, Colorado, records department and found a transaction regarding a land transfer and Marsha's new married name, Hinsdale*. He then put that name into a circular grid with Otero County as the center and got a phone number in Kansas and left a message. Marsha Egley Hinsdale called him back.

Brewer was hoping that the young girlfriend, whom Tom had left pregnant and alone in a hotel room in Helper, would now be a scorned ex-wife with details to share.

"You are welcome to waste your time driving out here. I'll invite you into my home, but I have nothing new to tell you." This is how Brewer remembered the conversation he had on the phone when she returned his call.

Sheriff Cordova approved their trip, and on October 11, 2009, Detectives Brewer and Taylor met with Tom's 1970 girlfriend Marsha at her residence in Kansas. Brewer asked Marsha to recall the night of Loretta's murder. She explained that she had fallen asleep watching television and was waiting for Tom to return home. She said she was awakened by Tom arriving home sometime between three and five a.m. She remembered being angry and asking him where he'd been, to which he only replied, "I'm here now." Marsha was seven months pregnant.

According to Marsha, Tom bathed in his clothes, put them in a bag, and then disposed of the bag the next day. When Marsha pressed for answers, asking Tom where he had been, he admitted he'd taken Loretta and her daughter out for hamburgers at the Arctic Circle. Tom said he was going to the local laundromat across the street from their hotel between ten and eleven the following day. Marsha found this odd, considering they usually did laundry on Sundays. Even more peculiar was the fact that upon Tom's return, he no longer possessed the bag of clothes he had taken to the laundromat and had been wearing the night before.

A few months after Loretta's murder, when Egley was released from jail, Marsha asked him about his involvement with the case. He claimed he had nothing to do with the crime and told her not to worry about it. Marsha said she always carried doubt in her mind after that. Not long before Egley was arrested, police came to the hotel and asked Egley for the clothes he'd worn that night. Although Tom gave the police a pair of jeans and a shirt, he later admitted to Marsha that he'd given them different clothes.

At this point, Brewer said, "I thought you had nothing to tell me."

She responded, "Oh, was that important?"

Marsha informed Detective Brewer that while Tom was being held in jail, she gave birth to their baby girl in mid-September of 1970, and they later moved to Rocky Ford, Colorado, sometime in January of 1971. During the interview, Marsha said she always suspected that he could have been responsible for Loretta's murder, and she never understood why he was released from jail. She believed they'd had enough evidence to keep him there.

As Brewer concluded Marsha's interview, he remembered a piece of wisdom Dr. Rachel Walton had shared with him regarding cracking cold cases: "Relationships change. Use it to your benefit." The words resonated deeply, emphasizing the evolving nature of people and their relationships. And he could use this as an investigative asset. As an example, Brewer emphasized that he was convinced Marsha knew more than she let on about Tom's involvement despite her original statement. But he understood that being pregnant, in a new town without any family or friends, and not even being able to drive to the store would make her protective of the only person she knew there, Tom. But after being divorced from Tom for many years, Marsha had nothing good to say about him and added he turned out to be a deadbeat dad. Brewer said talking to Marsha was like "opening a lost case file that he could finally look into." He felt he had found a pot of gold.

CHAPTER 14

NEXT STEPS

Next up on Detective Brewer's interview list was Barbara Battison (then Barbara Busio). Barbara owned the Sportsman Bar and had employed Tom Egley as a handyman. On the day after the murder, according to Barbara, she spotted Egley at the laundromat across the street from the bar. She realized he was washing clothes, and when she confronted him, he said he burned the clothes from "that" night. When Barbara pressed him, asking if the police wanted his clothes for evidence, Egley said, "I just gave them some other Levi's and a T-shirt."

Barbara said that Tom told her the police found fibers on his clothes, which matched the ones from Loretta Jones's home, but he said that they couldn't prove anything from those fibers because he'd already been to Loretta's house before the murder and had played on a rug with Loretta's daughter, Heidi.

According to Barbara, Sheriff Passic asked her to bring Marsha into the sheriff's office so Marsha could visit Egley. Sheriff Passic told Barbara they could use his office in hopes of recording Tom saying something incriminating. Barbara relayed to Brewer that when Tom came into Sheriff Passic's office for their visit, he said, "Shh, it's probably bugged."

According to Barbara, Tom also insisted they never caught him because he read books and magazines like *True Detective*, a claim Marsha confirmed. Barbara had visited their hotel room once and had seen stacks upon stacks of these magazines and said that Tom would talk about how a person could get away with a crime and often said it with an air of excitement in his tone.

Barbara added that Rudy SanFelice, the owner of the Newhouse Hotel in Helper where Tom lived, told her about a welder's-type hat Tom always wore. Tom had washed it after the murder and hung it out his apartment window to dry.

Detective Brewer sat down with Rudy on September 30, 2009, to hear his version of events. Rudy's mom and aunt ran the Highway Rendezvous, where they and the patrons saw Tom the night of the murder with blood on his clothing. Not long after that, Rudy said that the Helper chief of police, Bill Meyers, and Albert Passic told him that Tom was a suspect and asked Rudy to keep an eye on him. He also recalled the police deputies searching Tom's hotel room and discovering a knife with a narrowed blade, covered in blood, hidden in his room. That accusation was later questioned since no murder weapon had ever been connected to Egley.

Rudy recalled Sheriff Passic picking Egley up from the hotel for questioning. After he returned, Egley told Rudy, "They think I killed that girl in Price. What do you think?"

Rudy didn't answer the question and told Egley he could think what he wanted. A few days later, he was doing some plumbing work and sensed someone behind him. When Rudy turned around, Egley was holding a brakeman's club, a three-foot metal or wooden tool used by railroad workers. Feeling threatened, Rudy asked what Tom was doing, but he didn't reply. A few days later, Tom said, "I could have bashed your brains in if I wanted to." After that, every time Tom saw Rudy, Tom would say, "You think I did it, don't you?" Eventually, Rudy replied, "I know you did." And after a pause, Egley looked him in the eye and said, "Well, they're not going to prove it. They got to prove it first."

Detective Brewer's investigation continued, uncovering mostly information already known. The problem with cold cases is that even after reviewing witness reports and reinvestigating witnesses, detectives often land back at square one. Brewer knew he needed to continue investigating other measures to get a well-rounded perspective on everything that had happened back in 1970. Still, he wasn't prepared for exactly how many ups and downs there would be. He was tired and also under a lot of stress at work.

When Brewer was in his twenties, he bought his first guitar—a Takamine. Being self-taught, he liked to play rhythmic chords and sing Elvis songs. His favorite band of all time was the Beatles, but KISS made points in his book when they signed one of his guitars at a Vegas backstage meet and greet. "They put on a great show," he recalled.

When burdened by the weight of the world, Brewer would retreat to his quiet home office, mix up a drink, and find solace in the gentle strumming of his guitar. Music had a way of soothing his soul, as did a gin and tonic! Brewer knew in order to do his best work, he needed to walk away from the case and clear his head. Ideas (and possibly a headache) would come in the morning.

On September 15, 2009, Brewer and his partner, Detective Roger Taylor, went to the crime scene at 468 East 400 South, where Loretta had been murdered all those years ago. The house had new owners who allowed the detectives to look through the rooms.

The house looked relatively the same from the outside, except for a few landscape changes. It had been newly painted and was no longer coined "the creepy white house on the corner." Except for the new carpet on the living room floor, the room Loretta had died in looked the way it had back in 1970. The original linoleum floor remained underneath the carpet, and the new owners allowed Brewer to peel it back and look beneath it to search for trace evidence, but he found nothing.

The back of the house had undergone remodeling, which included updates to the kitchen and bathroom. Additional bedrooms were added, and the new owners replaced Heidi's bedroom door. Detective Brewer asked if, by chance, they still had the old door, and miraculously, they did. Brewer found it in a wood pile out behind the house. Not only did it match the door frame perfectly, but it also had the original vintage tin brass plate that housed both the knob and the ornate keyhole. The one that Heidi described looking through on the morning after the murder and seeing her mother's motionless body.

While in Colorado to interview Tom at a later time, Brewer made a second trip to Kansas to speak again with Marsha. He had some timing issues, and he wanted to have her clarify the case. When asked if she had married Tom while in Utah, she said that his attorney, Thorit Hatch, had encouraged her to marry him so that she would not have to testify against him. Mr. Hatch was a graduate of the University of Utah (1927) and practiced law in Helper for forty years, and Tom was lucky to have such an esteemed lawyer on his side. But Brewer had to ask himself . . . Why would an attorney for an innocent man give that kind of advice?

CHAPTER 15

STATEMENTS

D espite hitting one dead end after another, Detective Brewer persevered, fully aware of the challenging nature of such cases. He asked Loretta's three sisters to write out statements of who Heidi had said murdered her mother in hopes that the testimony of a four-year-old would be enough to take the case to court. After all, she was present at the scene, and she possibly knew the killer's identity. So despite the task's difficulty, the women wrote out their statements and remained hopeful that their discomfort would eventually pave the way for a breakthrough in the case.

May 1, 2009

To Whom It May Concern:

This is the most significant memory I have of my sister's murder: I was standing by the doorway into the living room from the hall in my mother's house. There were, I believe, two police officers questioning Heidi. I remember Heidi saying, "Tom did it. He hurt my mom."

Linda LuDeen Jones Parker

Loretta Jones Murder Case, death July 31, 1970

Loretta was a single mom living alone with her four-year-old daughter. She was my sister. Loretta received threatening phone calls a week before she was killed. She told our mother. Our mother told her to call the police. So she did call them. The police in Price told her they could not do anything unless something happened to her. I overheard this conversation between my mother and sister Loretta. [No evidence of this phone call was recovered from records, as all records from 1970 had been lost or destroyed.]

Loretta was murdered. Heidi was left at their home with her dead mother until sometime the next morning or afternoon when she told a neighbor boy she thought her mother was dead. She was there all night alone with a dead mother.

The sheriff contacted my dad at noon the next day. We were not allowed to pick up Heidi or have contact with her until that afternoon. Loretta was dating a man who was a truck driver named Bob Blackwell. They were thinking seriously about getting married. She didn't go to Moab with us because she was waiting for Bob to come see her that night. My father was a building contractor who had a warehouse by Loretta's house. He went down to get supplies that night with my brother Duane and sister-in-law Erma. They waved at Heidi and Loretta before going to the warehouse because they were outside on their back porch around nine p.m. When they left the warehouse, Loretta's lights were off at her house, and they assumed she had gone to bed. That was the last anyone in our family saw her alive.

The following police officers came to our home to question Heidi about her mom's murder. I was in the living room of my house when they questioned her. The officers' names were Bob Tilton, Albert Pas-

sic, and Art Poloni. When they questioned Heidi about who killed her mom, she always said and never changed any names. She always said Tom killed her mom. She saw Tom stab her mom, and she fell to the ground.

This is all I know that is factual; everything else that I know are theories and things that people have said to me.

Lila Stevens

December 21, 2009

Statement of my sister, Loretta Marie Jones' death:

My sister, Loretta Marie Jones, was murdered on July 30, 1970. A day or two later Albert Passic and Art Poloni, came to our house and asked my parents if they could ask my niece, Heidi Lynn Jones, some questions about her mother's death. I remember Heidi answering one of the questions, saying "Tom killed my mom."

Carolyn Kendall

Bryon also shared a vivid memory of police officers visiting the family house to converse with his parents. "Heidi was sitting on the floor, playing with her toys, just like a normal kid, and eavesdropping on the adult conversation. Suddenly, she blurted out, 'Tom did it,' and just kept playing with her stuff." He wondered why her spontaneous utterance was never used in court, considering she was such a bright little girl.

Bryon also believes the case went cold initially because of a lack of expertise in handling such intricate matters. Additionally, he found it deeply unsettling and unprofessional that the police officers deliberated upon the specifics of his sister's murder in the presence of a four-year-old child.

On September 30, 2009, Detective Brewer contacted Boyd Bunnell, who was the district attorney in 1970, but Bunnell had no recollection of the case—or any files. Things weren't looking good as the investigation wore on. From November 16–19, Brewer searched for all the witnesses who had testified in the preliminary hearing. However, Arthur Poloni, the Price police chief, and Carbon County sheriff Albert Passic were both deceased. On December 14, 2009, Detective Brewer met with the Utah State Medical Examiner's Office and was told they had no physical evidence from this case.

But someone did. Heidi Jones gave Brewer a box of beads that had been hanging in the doorway of Loretta's bedroom in 1970—only five feet away from where Loretta's body was found. She had saved them along with some of her mother's other things she salvaged from LuDeen's garage. The hope was that the beads still held DNA evidence that previous cops had missed. On December 14, 2009, Detective Brewer took them to the Utah State Crime Lab for testing, hoping to find blood from someone other than Loretta Jones. Theoretically, if the assailant had cut himself during the attack, he might have touched the decorative beads and left some blood evidence. While Brewer waited for the results, hoping it would result in some proof he could use to identify Tom Egley as the suspect, he continued interviewing people related to the case.

On December 16, 2009, he connected with Judge Tom Platis, the presiding judge in the preliminary hearings. Platis said the only evidence the prosecution brought before him against Tom Egley was a fiber found on his clothes that matched fibers from Loretta Jones's house. But because Tom had been in the house before, it was not enough to prove anything, and he decided not to take the case to trial.

On January 6, 2010, the Utah State Crime Lab contacted Detective Brewer to report that no blood evidence was found on the beads. This was another dead end.

Detective Brewer always felt that the Carbon County deputies who initially investigated Loretta's murder should've dug deeper. "They could have focused on the Kulow deal a little more." Furthermore, he thought they were headed in the right direction with the case but didn't follow leads. However, because of a lack of records in the 1970 case, Brewer couldn't know for certain exactly what actions the original detectives had taken. Hindsight is 20/20, and he didn't feel it fair to call their shots as an armchair quarterback. All he had to go on was what he knew they didn't do—and that was using Heidi to help them get information on her mother's murder.

On January 28, he contacted Lori Kulow Fenner (then Lori Kulow), the child who had nearly been the victim of the attempted abduction on the day Loretta Jones was murdered. He wanted to see how much she recalled about the incident. In Lori's words: "Several days after this, my brother Jimmy and I went to the jail in Price to identify another man they picked up [as a suspect] for the murder of Loretta Jones, to find out if he was the one who had grabbed me. It was hard to look through the screens, and I told them I didn't know if it was him. The thing I remember the most was his hat. It looked like a bucket hat with different colors."

On February 3, 2010, Detective Brewer contacted Lori's brother, Jim Kulow Jr.

Jim was twelve years old at the time of Lori's attempted kidnapping and was there the night Lori was assaulted. He remembered it being just before dark, around nine p.m., and recalled a similar-looking hat on the individual. Jim described it as multicolored, plaid, and round. Jim and his friends witnessed the same man about fifteen minutes before the assault, half a block south of their street. He had been sitting on the curb eating a hamburger. Lori would later recall the man had greasy hands and smelled of food grease.

Although Lori was unsure if she identified the man correctly, Jim recalled that they did pick the greasy-handed, hat-wearing man out of the lineup. After they pointed him out as the man who'd attempted to take Lori, the police informed him that the man, Tom Egley, was also suspected of murdering Loretta Jones.

Although court records indicate that Egley was indicted—and later released—for the murder of Loretta Jones, Detective Brewer suspected that he was actually arrested for Lori Kulow's attempted kidnapping. Brewer found no exact records other than a booking card and a photo of Tom that said he was arrested for "assault and battery." Heidi gave him the actual photo. It had been in LuDeen's stuff, and it was the first time Brewer had seen the photo. That would align him more clearly with Lori's attempted abduction instead of Loretta's murder. Egley appeared to have spent three months in jail for that crime. Then he was released and given a pretrial hearing for Loretta's murder. However, many records regarding how the case unfolded were missing.

Regardless, Tom Egley had walked free from a lack of evidence connecting him to the murder. He'd never come under investigation again for either Loretta Jones's murder or the attempted kidnapping of Lori Kulow. Case(s) closed.

Brewer opined, "They were obviously on the right track back then, but the odd part is they never used Heidi in the preliminary hearing. She was a great eyewitness who saw and heard some things. I know they interviewed her but didn't use her as a witness, which was a mistake."

There were probably many reasons Heidi wasn't allowed to testify in her mom's murder. First, she had not seen the actual murder. Her saying "Tom did it" offered only a four-year-old opinion without eyewitness facts. Secondly, she was a traumatized child and easily persuaded or influenced by what she was hearing around her. Thirdly, putting a child on the stand can be tricky because they can easily be led. Their statements are often unreliable because of their limited understanding of words and their meanings. There are many more reasons why one might not use a young child as a viable witness, but one can only speculate why her testimony was discounted.

Feeling somewhat defeated, Brewer reached out to an old friend and mentor, Vince Meister, a Utah attorney known for his involvement in high-profile cases like the Utah Kennecott Copper case, which had gone cold for fourteen years and was finally solved by forensic science and a paint chip. The case was featured on *Forensic Files*—Season 12, Episode 29—"Guarded Secrets." The suspect in the case had come to the attention of the Carbon County Sheriff's Office many years later, and it brought Vince and a team of investigators to Price, where Brewer met Vince for the first time. "He sees things more as a detective than an attorney. He's a smart guy," complimented Brewer. The Carbon County case was never solved, but Meister became very interested in Loretta's cold case.

Vince listened intently as Brewer filled him in on the investigation, detailing the dead ends and challenges he had encountered. When Brewer replaced the phone in its cradle, he felt a renewed sense of purpose and confidence, thanks to the encouragement and guidance of his confidant. The camaraderie among officers was usually high. However, within his own department, instead of rallying behind Brewer's efforts to solve the cold case, there was reluctance and even opposition. The lack of support from his colleagues left Brewer feeling isolated and frustrated, highlighting the breakdown of trust and solidarity within their close-knit group, but he could always count on Vince.

Strengthened by the phone conversation, Brewer knew there was one person who had the answers—an individual who would most likely lie but who could potentially provide valuable information that could change everything. He would take that next step.

CHAPTER 16

A History of Violence

Among the suspects in the case of Loretta Jones was Mr. Thomas Edward Egley, born July 6, 1940, in Model, Colorado, to Glen T. and Mary E. Egley. Model is an abandoned unincorporated village in Las Animas County, Colorado. The Model post office was in operation from 1912 to 2021 and was the last business or service standing there for many years. The community initially was a "planned" or "model" community, hence the name. The young couple lived on a farm with Glen's parents, William L. and Anna B. Egley, and their other children, three sons and one daughter. According to the April 1, 1940, census, Glen worked as a farmhand, the same occupation as his father. The record indicates that Glen was born in Colorado and completed his eighth year in school, whereas Mary was born in Oklahoma and attended school only until her third year. Because the census was taken in April, Mary would have been approximately six months pregnant with her first child, Tom.

A news article from *The Home Journal* dated April 1955 shows a black-and-white photo of two smiling children dressed in their Sunday best. Under the photo is the following paragraph, "Introducing . . . Edward and Carolyn Egley. Edward will soon be 15 and Carolyn is 12. They have adjusted themselves so well in our family and we are happy that we could find room for them. Children in a good, happy, Christian environment soon forget their unfortunate past and it is a joy to see their growth and development into good Christian men and women. They came to live with us in March." The paper was addressed to Mrs. Ray Williams, 693 S. Fifth St., Rocky Ford, Colorado, but it is unknown as to who the children went to live with, as the article does not state any names. Were they adopted out to another family or taken into foster care for a short time? Mrs. Ray Williams is Mary, the children's biological mother, who later divorced Glen and married Ray Williams.

Most of Tom's life was spent growing up in and then later moving back to Rocky Ford, Colorado, which is about sixty miles north of Model in Otero County. Rocky Ford is a small town famous for its cantaloupes and watermelons due to its soil content and temperature fluctuation, which provide great growing conditions. As of the 2020 census, it boasted a population of 3,876.

Little information is available regarding Tom Egley's childhood. His sister, Carolyn, now deceased, likely had the closest connection to Tom during their formative years. Any friends who might have known him in the forties and fifties are also assumed to have passed away. He did have one friend in Rocky Ford with whom he attended school, and they shared a birthday. His location is unknown. Military records list Tom's highest level of education as "High School—9."

Standing at five feet, eight inches, with brown hair and blue eyes, Tom had sleek features, a long pointed nose, and slicked-back hair. Some would call him a ladies' man, consistently juggling a handful of women.

Tom enlisted in the Navy in 1957, when he was seventeen. He was stationed at USNAF Litchfield Park, Phoenix, Arizona. Records indicate he was discharged as a seaman apprentice and only served for nine months and eighteen days. Code 260 was listed as the reason for his discharge—"Unsuitability, inaptitude." Typed in 13a, Character of Service box, was the word *Honorable*. Because his length of service was short, he was not entitled to veterans' benefits. It was here that he probably got his first tattoo. A girl's head and a rose appeared on his upper right arm, a small heart and a set of wings on his lower left arm, and the name "Tom" and an eagle were inked on his lower right arm.

It seemed that Egley first attracted the attention of law enforcement in 1965. He married Shirley Evans* on April 27, 1961, in Denver, Colorado, and they later moved to Reno, Nevada. It was here that Shirley, then twenty-two years old, first called the police on her husband, Tom, who was twenty-four.

Upon arriving at their residence at 4:20 p.m. on May 17, 1965, Tom was nowhere to be found. Officers discovered the house in disarray. According to their notes, everything on the kitchen table was tossed to the floor, and other items around the house, like their dog's bed, had been moved around.

Shirley explained that Tom had knocked her around during an argument. Shirley was advised this was a civil matter and that she would need to consult with her attorney. The call was listed as a "family argument" instead of a domestic disturbance. However, just over an hour later, at 5:45 p.m., officers returned to the house and arrested Tom Egley for domestic battery.

He called Shirley from the police station on May 18 and placed a second call on May 19 to his mother, Mary Williams, who lived in Rocky Ford, Colorado. Records were unclear as to who bailed him out. However, on February 15, 1966, when Egley was living back in Rocky Ford, Colorado, and was arrested for attempted burglary, his mother, Mary Williams, was listed as the surety for his bail.

Tom was acquitted of the attempted burglary. His rap sheet also included two bounced checks and a DUI in Elko, Nevada, in 1990, resulting in a revoked license. Sometime between 1966 and 1970, he moved to Helper, Utah, a small town six miles north of Price. Between 1971 and 1982, Tom was married three or four other times and was divorced for the last time in 1984. His pattern of behavior, as reported by his ex-wives, of using and abusing women, was indicative of the type of person he was and the type of man he would become.

Regarding Tom's paternity, the precise count of his children remains uncertain, as he might have other children with women who have not been named. Currently, two daughters and one son have been identified.

Lauren* was born in 1964 during Tom's marriage to Shirley while they resided in Colorado. Shirley had two other older children, but they were not Tom's. Lauren affirmed that she only discovered Tom was her father when she was sixteen years old and her mother took her and her sister to a funeral, presumably that of Tom's father. Lauren was uncertain if it was Glen or Ray. Shirley remained in contact with Tom's sister, Carolyn, a hairstylist, and Lauren assumed that this connection led to their awareness of the funeral. Despite Carolyn often doing the girls' hair, they were never informed that she was their aunt; instead, they believed she was just a close friend of their mother's.

After the funeral, they visited a house Lauren thought belonged to Tom's parents. Tom opened the door and declared, "I'm your father." Her only response was a simple "hey" while her sister left the room. Recollecting the meeting, Lauren recalled sitting at a long table with Tom, who was accompanied by a girl she assumed was the woman he moved to Utah with. This singular encounter remained their only meeting, although she did receive a Christmas card from him one year. Lauren does not believe her two older siblings are Tom's children, and their family avoids discussing the matter entirely. She has not undergone a DNA test and is unaware of any half-siblings. Her mother is unwilling to discuss the subject, and Lauren is content to leave it be. A book could be written about Lauren's life, as she has gone through some rough times herself. She's content with living near her children and enjoys watching her grandchildren grow up.

Regarding Tom's second child, a clip in the *Sun Advocate* in September 1970 announced the couple's news: "Mr. and Mrs. Thomas Egley of Helper, a baby girl." Tom was unable to attend the birth of his daughter, Mary, due to his being incarcerated for the attempted abduction of ten-year-old Lori Kulow on the same day that Loretta Jones was murdered.

Mary, named after her grandmothers on both sides, was born in Price and lived with Tom Egley and Marsha at the Newhouse Hotel. She was too young to know when they moved to Colorado; however, her mother told her that she and Tom stayed together for two to three years to try to make it work for Mary's sake. As a child, she visited Tom only on weekends, but her mom put a stop to the visits because Tom was drinking heavily.

Mary loved her dad. The last time she saw Tom, her own child was about three months old. They had stopped in Rocky Ford with some of her family for a planned visit to see her mom's mother, Mary (not Tom's mother, who was also named Mary). But they also drove by Tom's mother's trailer, and they saw an old van parked there, so she asked if they could stop and see that grandmother (Tom's mom). She remembers knocking, and Tom answered the door.

"Is my grandma here?" she timidly asked.

"No," Tom answered crudely, "she died three fucking years ago." Tom added, "You must be Mary."

And she answered, "You must be Tom."

He was fat and just "nasty," unlike the way she remembered him. Her recollection of him was of a very handsome younger man. She possessed a photograph of her sitting on his lap, about which she said, "He is just gorgeous."

Before they left the trailer, she asked him why he had never tried to contact her or had anything to do with her. She knew her grandmother had her contact information, but looking back now, she states, "I know why . . . You've been on the run for fifty freaking years. You were afraid that if you came out of hiding, they would arrest you because you hadn't paid child support." (One entry in Tom's records indicates that on January 18, 1979, there was an attempt to locate him by the Kansas Department of Social Services, where Marsha was then living, as per their child support laws, but whether or not they were successful in getting child support was not noted.)

She again asked, "Why didn't you look for me or try to call me?"

"I just didn't want to be bothered by you kids," was his cold answer. It hurt.

Mary was aware that Tom had married after he and Marsha divorced in 1976, but one day, while staying at her step-grand-mother's, she went to take the trash out, and the next-door neighbor was doing the same. Mary smiled and said, "Hello," but the woman turned pale and asked, "Are you Tom Egley's daughter?" That was the day she learned of Thomas Egley Jr., her half brother. Thomas Egley Jr., or Tommy, born in 1976, lived intermittently with his grandmother and Tom throughout his teen years. Rosemarie, the neighbor, then introduced her-self as Tom Jr.'s mother. Mary did not meet her half brother that day, but he showed up on her step-grandmother's porch months later dressed totally in black, wearing black lipstick and fingernail polish. They talked for a few hours. She heard later that he had moved out of the area. Mary tried to keep in contact but only heard back from him twice.

When Brewer interviewed Rosemarie, she was asked if she had ever been frightened of Tom. She visibly paled and hesitated to answer until prompted. She recalled an unsettling incident when she and Tom had been at home watching TV when their two dogs started barking incessantly. Tom, without hesitation, grabbed his pistol, went outdoors, and shot both dogs. Upon returning inside, he instructed her to "go clean it up." "He was a hothead and could snap easily," she added.

Mary said her father, Tom, moved around until after his mother died, and then he settled in her Rocky Ford single-wide trailer. Mary didn't remember Tom being violent, but she re-called a traumatic night when she was three or four years old on her visitation weekend. Tom and a girlfriend took her to the outside picture show and told her to lie down in the back and try to sleep. He had taken them to see *The Exorcist*. Mary claimed she had to have therapy because it scared her so badly.

Mary ended the interview positively by sharing that she had three wonderful daughters and thirteen amazing grandsons and spent most of her days at home with her spoiled dogs. Although her mother suffered a stroke and has disability issues, they remain close.

"Come check out the Rocky Ford fair sometime. It has the best watermelon and cantaloupe around."

CHAPTER 17

Meeting Egley

On March 16, 2010, Detective David Brewer pulled into a tree-lined driveway in Rocky Ford, Colorado, and parked next to an old white van sitting next to a mailbox and a squat chain-link fence that delineated the property. The single-wide trailer was enclosed by a wall made from bicycle wheels that formed a barrier around the front of the residence. Adjacent to the property, an old Ford truck was parked behind a gate. Rusty gym equipment was scattered in the tall grass and a "Beware of Dog" sign served as a cautionary notice to trespassers.

The number 20454 on the gate was the address on the county road where seventy-year-old Thomas Edward Egley called home. Forty years had passed since Loretta Jones had been murdered. At that time, Tom Egley had lived without any investigators showing up at his door. He wasn't famous; he hadn't written any memoirs people would read. He didn't have a huge family or an established career with honors achieved and a gold watch at retirement.

If he was the man responsible for Loretta's murder—as Heidi Jones believed—then Detective Brewer wanted to ensure that Egley's days living as a free man would be numbered.

Brewer and his partner, Detective Taylor, were greeted by Tom Egley at the front door. He was much older than his mugshots, frail, and slightly hunched in his five-foot-eight frame. His brown hair had grayed, and his blue eyes were murky. Brewer explained he wanted to talk to him about events that occurred back in Carbon County in 1970. Tom agreed, and when Brewer asked if there was a more comfortable place to chat, Tom invited the two men into his home.

Brewer and Taylor took a seat on the musty couch in the living room while Tom sat closest to the door. Usually, officers stationed themselves closest to an exit, but they weren't worried about Tom as a threat. Tom asked the two deputies, "What's the problem?" and Brewer responded by asking Tom if he had any idea why they would be there today. Tom stated that one of his ex-girlfriends in Carbon County had been killed some years earlier. He said he was arrested for the murder but was subsequently released and hadn't had any further troubles with the law since then.

He said he couldn't remember the girl's name. And yet he remembered that he had spent about sixty days in jail waiting for his court date. When asked why he'd been released, Tom said he thought it was because the arresting officer had been away at school. He explained that he'd been living in Helper during the time of the murder. Still, it hadn't stopped the cops from taking him to the sheriff's office repeatedly for questioning.

During one such session in 1970, the cops asked Tom if he would take a polygraph. Tom initially agreed. However, two weeks later, the officers explained they had the polygraph ready for him, but he would have to take it in Salt Lake City, not Price. That was when Tom changed his mind and refused to take the polygraph, and he was arrested.

Detective Brewer sat back, listening in earnest. He didn't know exactly what to believe about what this man said. He was disadvantaged because much of the evidence from the seventies had been destroyed, and many witnesses were deceased. However, there was one fact Brewer knew that Tom either ignored or overlooked.

According to the information Detective Brewer uncovered, Tom's criminal record indicated that he had been arrested for battery, not for Loretta's murder. In addition, Brewer explained to Tom that he had been identified through a lineup as the individual who attempted to abduct Lori Kulow, who was ten years old.

Tom shook his head and denied what Brewer was telling him. "That's way out of my league," he said, referring to the attempted kidnapping. He insisted that he had never been in a lineup and had no knowledge of this battery charge.

It was unclear to Brewer if Tom was making this up or if he'd buried the memory from so long ago. Perhaps he honestly didn't remember why he'd been arrested.

Detective Taylor asked Tom to name the people he knew when he lived in Helper, hoping it would get him talking. Tom explained that he lived at the Helper Newhouse Hotel for about a year with his then-girlfriend Marsha and occasionally tended the bar for Rudy SanFelice. Tom also said he sprayed weeds for the city, but what brought him to Helper in the first place was working on microwave towers and for the phone company. He put himself in Helper about 1971–1972 and then moved back to Rocky Ford and started working for Highline Canal.

Some of this information confirmed Detective Brewer's prior findings, and some of it he was hearing for the first time. It didn't give him much else to go on, and Brewer's natural inclination as a detective was to prove innocence by eliminating the possibility of guilt. And yet, hearsay, forty years after Loretta's murder, would be unlikely to stand up in court.

He needed more. Something more than just his gut feeling that Tom Egley wasn't telling the truth. He needed something solid.

He was curious: How had Tom first met Loretta Jones?

A mutual friend, Tom explained, someone whose name he couldn't recall. And yet, without hesitation, he quickly added that he and Loretta hadn't dated long. Maybe less than a month. Tom's reason? Loretta was too much of a hippie for him, too much into reincarnation. He thought she was weird.

He knew she had a daughter, but Heidi's name evaded him like so much else. He added that it was rare for him to go to Loretta's house to see her. Instead, she would visit his room at the hotel.

According to Tom, Marsha came out to Helper to be with him shortly after he broke off relations with Loretta. Marsha was already pregnant and ultimately had their child while he was in jail.

At this point in the interview, Detective Brewer couldn't deny the fact that Tom seemed agitated. He had begun to pace the floor and was smoking one cigarette after another. Taylor had also noticed and asked Tom if it bothered him that they were here talking about his past, about Loretta.

Tom admitted it did bother him, not because he was guilty of a crime but because he never thought this would be brought up again. The past was over.

Brewer nodded along, yet it was becoming clear that Tom Egley was too arrogant for his own good. He was either innocent or a murderer, and Brewer was beginning to get a pretty good idea of which was true.

Brewer dove in headfirst, hoping a direct question would push Tom over the edge. Did Tom remember going to Loretta's house on the night she was murdered? Tom shook his head. He didn't remember. He said Marsha was at the hotel with the baby, contradicting his earlier statement that she was pregnant the night in question.

Taylor chimed in, "Have you ever been to her house?"

Without blinking, Tom said, "No, I haven't."

It was a bold lie that differed from everything Brewer had heard from witnesses who insisted Tom said he'd never be found guilty because fibers from his clothes were already in the house.

Not only that, but from the limited evidence Brewer had, he knew that this same fiber argument was part of Tom's defense that helped get him released.

Detective Brewer went along with it.

For now.

So, what did Tom remember from that night?

Tom answered easily. He'd gotten something to eat in Price and then taken a ride home with his friend. It had been dark out by the time he left. He couldn't recall the name of the person who'd given him a ride but thought maybe it was McBride. This was the first time Brewer had heard this name.

If he got a ride, how did he arrive in Price?

Tom hitchhiked. Did it whenever he needed a ride.

Taylor leaned forward. Did Tom remember what he ate for dinner the night of the murder?

He nodded. The man who couldn't recall the names of his friends answered quickly. He'd bought a hamburger at the Arctic Circle drive-in. In fact, he remembered sitting on the curb to eat his burger.

Egley's response sent a shiver down Detective Brewer's spine.

It was astonishing! The fact that Egley recalled such a minute detail indicated to Brewer that there was much more etched in Egley's memory. Moreover, Tom's positioning on the curb, precisely where the Kulow kids spotted him, added significant importance to the revelation.

When Tom realized nothing was happening in Price that night, he decided to head back home to Helper.

Brewer asked Tom why he thought he was a suspect in Loretta's murder to begin with. Tom said a woman he had dated before Loretta had given the police his name.

It was Brewer's turn to drop the bombshell. He locked eyes with Egley and explained that during his preliminary hearings forty years earlier, the prosecution presented fiber evidence against him. The fiber was found on Tom's pants, linking him to Loretta's home.

Tom explained that the fiber had been on his clothes because he had been in Loretta's home before. Brewer confronted Tom with his earlier lie and asked, "How many times had you been to Loretta's home?"

"Not that many times," Tom responded. "More than once. But not more than five times."

"Do you know how Loretta was murdered?" Taylor asked.

"I don't," Tom responded.

Brewer clasped his hands. "Tom. Do you know what DNA is?"

Tom nodded. "I do."

Brewer's heart pounded steadily as the room became eerily quiet. Could this be the moment he'd get a confession out of Tom?

Brewer took a breath. "The medical examiner took some vaginal swabs samples from Loretta, and semen was found. Is there any reason your DNA would be on those swabs?"

Tom shrugged. "Not that I can think of."

Brewer wasn't ready to back down. "Is it possible you had sexual intercourse with Loretta the night of her murder before you left her house?"

Tom denied the allegations.

If Brewer could link Tom to the house that night, he'd have something, an inch he could turn into a mile.

"Maybe," Brewer continued, "you had sex with Loretta that night, left her home, and got a ride back to Helper with your friends."

Tom adamantly shook his head. "I just don't remember having sex with her that night."

Taylor cleared his throat. "How about this? If we set up a polygraph to confirm everything you're saying, would you be willing to take one?"

"No."

It wasn't surprising to Brewer that Tom refused to take a polygraph, but he knew it was worth the shot.

Taylor nodded. "Tom, what do you think should happen to the person responsible for Loretta's death? Even if it was thirty-nine years ago."

Tom pursed his lips. "That person should go to jail."

Taylor continued. "Even after all this time has passed? You think they should still go to jail?"

Tom shrugged. "I couldn't tell ya that." Tom chewed his bottom lip. "It depends on whether he's done it again or not."

His answer hung in the air. It depends on whether he's done it again or not! Had Brewer heard that correctly? What kind of response was that? An innocent person would probably respond yes. A guilty person might qualify his answer to necessitate additional crime, suggesting a life of criminal activity. This was precisely the moment Brewer knew he was in the presence of Loretta's killer. Up until this moment, he had kept an open mind about Tom's involvement, but that statement left nothing open for interpretation.

Beyond that, was Tom inadvertently implying that whoever had killed Loretta had murdered others? Could Tom be a serial killer?

Brewer studied Tom. "Loretta's four-year-old daughter told police at the time that the person who had killed her mom was you. Why do you think she would do that?"

Tom shook his head. "Because I'd been there before, and she knew my name."

"But her daughter insisted that you were at their house that night," Brewer continued. "The night Loretta was killed."

Tom's features remained emotionless. "I have no idea."

Another lie, but it was time for Brewer to move forward and take a different approach.

He asked Tom if he knew Barbara Busio from back then. Tom stated he didn't and that Rudy SanFelice was his boss.

"There are a lot of witnesses that have details about this case," Brewer explained. "Details that aren't in your favor. New details, in fact. Certain things that didn't come to light in 1970. There's been a lot of advancement in DNA technology since the seventies. They test DNA swabs."

Did Brewer have him? Would this be it?

Tom clasped his hands together. "Well, I don't remember having sex with her."

"That night?" Detective Brewer asked.

Tom glared at him. "I sure don't. Ain't saying I didn't, but I don't remember it. I always thought they'd caught the guy that murdered Loretta."

Brewer smiled. "Not yet."

Tom nodded. "Well, I'm not too worried about it because I know I didn't do it."

The interview ended, and although Brewer hadn't gotten the concrete evidence he'd hoped to, his conversation with Tom had eliminated all doubt in his mind. Tom might have convinced himself all these years later that he could rewrite the past to make himself believe he hadn't killed Loretta, but that wouldn't change the fact.

Heidi was right. Brewer knew he had just spoken to her mother's murderer. And now he needed to figure out how exactly he would prove it.

CHAPTER 18

The Seminar

E ven though David Brewer was now confident Tom Egley had killed Loretta Jones, he needed proof. He also needed support. Brewer was promoted to sergeant in 2012, but the case stalled for a bit. Then, after the Carbon County sheriff put him in charge of the detective unit, he received an email about an upcoming cold case seminar that invited officers to submit their cases to be reviewed in class. Sgt. Brewer was intrigued. He registered for the workshop and submitted Loretta's case. He was surprised when he heard back that his case had been chosen.

This was a very busy time for Brewer. He had remarried in 2011, and the couple welcomed a baby girl. Diapers and chaos at home, new responsibilities at work, and the cold case always present in the background. He had been elected for the fifth time as Master of the Lodge. Like many family men before him, he was a member of the Masonic Fraternity. The teachings of freemasonry enjoin morality, charity, and obedience to the law of the land and belief in brotherhood and helping others. Brewer was key in organizing the Carbon Lodge bowling tournament to raise money for the local Children's Justice Center. Brewer found comfort and camaraderie at the monthly fellowship meetings, a sense of connection that was notably absent among his colleagues at the sheriff's office.

Still, he managed to juggle all his priorities with steadfast determination and felt he could squeeze in time to attend the seminar.

Brewer presented the case very nervously to a class of over a hundred police officers. He remembered being irritated at the number of questions being asked. Did you do this? Did you ask that? He felt they were questioning his detective skills, not realizing that the case had started decades after the murder and most of the players were deceased, and of course, he tried this and that! However, he felt this seminar was the turning point for the case because it validated a turn in the case he wanted to explore.

Ben Pender, of the Unified Police Department, Salt Lake City, asked Sgt. Brewer if he had thought of exhuming the body. Brewer explained that up until the victim's mother, LuDeen Jones, passed away, it was not an option the family would approve. Technically, LuDeen was the body's custodian because Heidi was legally adopted, making her Loretta's sister, not her daughter. Brewer said that now Heidi could legally permit her mother's body to be exhumed.

The class agreed it would be a good time to rethink the possibility of obtaining DNA from the remains. Brewer, however, voiced his concerns about the odds of finding anything with a case this old. Experts told him it was a slim chance, and the conditions had to be just right. But then, what did he have to lose?

A woman attending the seminar who worked at an independent lab shared with the class that there was a very good possibility that semen might be present that would still be usable for testing. Although in 1970, testing wasn't available, coroners would still do what they called "preserve the jar," which meant keeping the vaginal area intact and undisturbed by not adding embalming fluids or chemicals. Brewer had not thought of that but was primarily interested in fingernails and the jewelry (rings), hoping they would have traces of DNA. He recalled watching a documentary about a soldier who died in Vietnam. Thirty years later, when the soldier's body was exhumed, it looked as if he had just been buried, unchanged by time. This is what Sgt. Brewer was hoping for.

Ben Pender suggested that if exhumation failed for DNA retrieval, the next step was to mislead the suspect by announcing a discovery to the media. *Brilliant*, Brewer thought.

Sgt. Brewer was hopeful, but the odds were against him. It is estimated that there are more than 250,000 unsolved homicides in the United States, many of which date back decades. Advances in technology and DNA analysis have led to increased success in solving cold cases in recent years. The National Institute of Justice reports that DNA evidence has been used to advance forensics—scientific tests or techniques to help solve a crime—as the primary means of solving these cases.

However, to get a conviction, Dr. Walton reminded him, it would also require "good old-fashioned shoe leather involving interviews and interrogation methods."

From the outset, Brewer encountered a challenging situation and perceived that the county attorney obstructed his efforts to seek justice. The constant response he got from that office was that there wasn't sufficient evidence to bring charges; they needed more. When Jeff Wood was elected sheriff, he permitted Brewer full authority to investigate the cold case in order to get the "more" he needed.

Brewer felt they needed a new perspective on the case, one they had never considered before. He and the sheriff wondered if the answers could lie in the one person they had yet to approach—the one who'd died at the hands of her killer. So, with some consideration, they decided that exhuming Loretta Jones's body and getting the media involved could shed light and give them the necessary answers to jump-start the case to resolve it.

But what would Heidi think? Digging up her mom's body, doing another autopsy, consulting with a medical examiner. Would it be too much?

Sgt. Brewer ran it past Heidi.

Her response?

"Give me a shovel, and I'll help dig."

CHAPTER 19

LUCK OR FATE

S gt. Brewer might not outwardly admit he believed in good luck charms, but the small silver leprechaun that hung on his rearview mirror might suggest otherwise. To some, it might just be a funny little guy, but to others, it's a talisman, something that can create positive energy and protection for its possessor, much like a cross or an evil eye. The good luck charm had once belonged to Loretta Jones, and having it made him feel a deeper connection to her. Heidi, who had given him the charm early on in the investigation, added an extra layer of significance to the already poignant item connected to this cold case. However, Brewer did have some odd OCD tendencies that may be called superstitions by some. "If I spill the salt, I toss some over my shoulder, and I am all about even numbers. If I come to the end of an M&M bag and the last one is an odd number, I throw it away." However, psychics are a different matter altogether.

During the investigation, there arose a difference in opinion between Detective Brewer, a skeptic who didn't put stock in psychics or superstitions, and a woman who held firm beliefs in such matters. While Brewer relied on traditional investigative methods and hard evidence, Heidi brought a unique perspective, suggesting that avenues beyond the tangible could lead to breakthroughs in the case. Despite their contrasting viewpoints, both were driven by a shared goal: to uncover the truth and bring justice to Loretta.

When facing the inevitable uncertainty of death, there's a curiosity about what comes afterward. Some pray to God so they can go to heaven, others meditate to connect with their soul, and some question who or what they will become when they're reincarnated.

These beliefs and practices can offer comfort, hope, and a sense of connection to something beyond the material world, providing solace in the face of mortality's enigmatic nature. Regardless of the diverse beliefs held by individuals, the quest to understand death and find meaning in it remains a fundamental aspect of the human experience.

And it's often the reason why people visit psychics/mediums to connect with those on the other side. It's part of a quest to discover that death is not the end but a transition to a different state of existence.

Psychics and mediums claim to have the ability to communicate with spirits or gain insights into the unknown. Some individuals turn to psychics or spiritual advisers in search of closure, reassurance, or guidance on how to deal with the loss of a loved one. While the legitimacy of such practices is debated, the desire to seek answers from beyond the tangible world reflects the human longing for understanding and connection with the deceased.

It was February 4, 2014, and Heidi was stuck in a limbo of sorts. Although she worked tirelessly to honor her mother's life by pursuing the person who killed her, Heidi grappled with profound questions. What happened to the soul? Where was her mom now?

A friend of Heidi's, Twila Martak (deceased), had gone to a "spiritual connection" event and wondered if it was something that could benefit Heidi. Heidi recalled the John Edwards events she had attended in California and how it had comforted her. So Heidi took her friend's advice and arranged to meet with a psychic medium, Lana Preston*, who shared space at the Southeastern Integrative Center of Healing Arts in Price.

Lana requested Heidi's presence at the house where her mother had tragically been murdered all those years before. Twila drove Heidi to the location, with Lana following closely in her own vehicle. They paused for a few moments outside the house, allowing Lana to attune herself to the home's aura. Afterward, the trio reconvened at the healing center for Heidi's first meeting with the visionary.

Heidi recounted that it didn't take long for Loretta's spirit to come through during her first reading. There were many things said, enough that Heidi couldn't deny that it really did feel like her mother's spirit. At one point, Loretta's spirit told her that "the cake is still in the pan." Loretta, who dabbled in baking, had made Heidi a cake more than once in her life, but this sounded more specific and reminded Heidi of something she'd recalled when working with Detective Brewer.

Not long after Brewer became involved with the case, he wanted to see if he could wean any new information out of Heidi's memory from the night of her mother's murder. The interview technique he used is called reverse chronological or reverse order questioning, which takes advantage of how memory works.

When people recall events in reverse order, they must think more deeply about each step. Another way to think about it is to recite the alphabet forward and then backward. You'll have to think about it more in reverse, forcing your mind to go back to what you know, or in this case, what Heidi experienced the night of the murder.

Often, reverse chronological questioning can lead to the victim having a more accurate recollection of details. It's also a way for law enforcement to prevent witnesses, victims, or suspects, for that matter, from creating fabricated stories, as it can be more challenging to come up with a story or to express a rehearsed story when asked to recall it in an unfamiliar sequence. Reversing the order of events can reveal inconsistencies or hidden details that might not be apparent when remembering events chronologically. It's often used in homicide investigations when gathering information to help solve a case.

When Heidi recalled the events of the night of the murder in reverse, she remembered one specific new detail: her mother had been in the process of baking a cake, something alluded to in her psychic reading. This cake pan was also mentioned in an earlier statement from Madalene C. Williams, who in 2008 said, "The home was locked up, and everything was left as it was for several years, including a cake on the cupboard."

After LuDeen, Heidi's grandmother, passed away, Heidi sifted through her belongings in the garage and stumbled upon items belonging to Loretta.

In a rush to prepare the abandoned home for new residents, everything had been swiftly boxed up and stored, remaining untouched for many years.

To Heidi's astonishment, she discovered the cake pan with its contents of dry crumbs still nestled within, preserved by the passage of time. Each morsel held the echoes of so many wonderful memories. As Heidi gazed upon it, she couldn't help but feel a rush of nostalgia, transported back to a time when laughter filled the air.

Another item of interest Heidi found among her mother's belongings were some notes scrawled on an envelope. Written in pencil by her mother's hand and dated July 27, 1970, was the following:

6—yes when you work instead of wish
10—yes if that one's certain of your love
24—an unexpected demand that must be met

For decades, Olive Nelson, a small-framed, silver-haired woman, held the revered title of the town's psychic sage. With lines etched like fine grooves into her weathered face, she exuded an air of ancient wisdom. Her piercing gaze seemed to penetrate the very depths of one's soul, leaving visitors feeling exposed yet strangely comforted. LuDeen and Loretta, drawn by the magnetic pull of her reputation, became devout regulars and would often join Mrs. Nelson at her kitchen table to have her read their cards or tea leaves.

Heidi discovered that her mother had had a tarot card reading done by Mrs. Nelson just three days before her tragic death, and Loretta had jotted the notes from that meeting on the envelope. The cryptic words left Heidi intrigued, and she wondered what significance they held for her mother and what secrets they might reveal about her past. The meaning of the numbers was uncertain, but the words next to twenty-four gave Heidi pause. Was it a premonition or a warning signaling the impending tragedy?

After Loretta's death, Mrs. Nelson informed Lila that Loretta had asked for a card reading on the day of her murder, but Mrs. Nelson, feeling something was not right, declined her request.

CHAPTER 20

PREMONITIONS AND NEAR DEATH

O ver the two-hour-long reading with the psychic medium Lana, Heidi had received enough messages from her mom to walk away with a new sense of clarity and peace. Loretta's absence had haunted Heidi, clinging to her like a shadow, a black hole of uncertainty. The reading assured Heidi of an afterlife and that her mother lived on. It was a relief for Heidi to know that her mother hadn't just evaporated into nothingness. Loretta's spirit had moved on to another realm, where she still existed, just in another form.

The house had picked up a presence and a conflict of emotions, including some images. The innocent-looking house had borne witness to a violent scene, its once serene atmosphere now tainted by the echoes of chaos and turmoil.

There was something about a skeleton key, the image of a keyhole, and if Heidi had any lingering doubts regarding the spirit world, they vanished then and there. It was a keyhole that Heidi peered out of the next morning, the one she squinted through to see her mother's lifeless body on the living room floor. The psychic had seen it too.

Two symbols appeared regularly in her readings: butterflies and hearts. Lana presented Heidi with a heart-shaped rose quartz crystal. Heart symbols were special to Heidi because, like good luck charms, Heidi associated them with messages from her mother. And after all, Heidi was born on Valentine's Day.

Heidi walked away from her first appointment with Lana with a new understanding of life and death—and a new ally. They had made a connection during the reading, and their conversations continued after the hour had passed. Eventually, they became friends, and Heidi gained another supporter in her quest to solve her mother's cold case and find the culprit who had killed Loretta Jones.

But could someone with intuitive abilities tell her the name of the murderer? Could Loretta's spirit offer information from beyond the grave that could solve her own case? It seemed far-fetched, but Heidi, now a believer in the existence of something more than just the physical realm, couldn't write it off as completely impossible.

At this point in their relationship, Brewer had a good understanding of Heidi's determined nature. Brewer's openness to Heidi's approach reflected his commitment to solving the case and his willingness to explore all possible avenues, even if they might seem unconventional or "hokey." Psychics and their critics differ sharply in their views about their usefulness, but Heidi believed that she had nothing to lose by eliciting the help and expertise of her new clairvoyant friend. Brewer knew that the usefulness of psychics in police investigations was controversial. However, psychics have long been and will undoubtedly continue to be involved in unsolved criminal investigations, so Brewer went along.

For Heidi, one thing was certain: Loretta Jones had saved the life of her four-year-old daughter the night she'd lost her own. Sometime during the investigation, this revelation became clear to Heidi. She couldn't shake the overwhelming feeling that her mother hoped and prayed she would stay safe in her room. Loretta's silent response to the brutal attack, despite the pain, spoke volumes about a mother's love and sacrifice. Loretta's restraint in crying out might explain why Heidi did not remember any sounds coming from outside her bedroom door. Even the police suspected that Loretta had stayed as quiet as possible so she wouldn't wake her daughter and alert her assailant to the presence of a possible eyewitness. "My mom was my hero that night, and I owed it to her to be her hero and bring her justice." That was what pushed Heidi forward in the pursuit of finding her mother's killer.

As Heidi continued investigating her mother's cold case, her psychic friend Lana and Lana's sister, Donna*, accompanied her to meet with Gene Strate, the county attorney in Price. A large binder filled with case records was on the corner of his desk. The visionary put her hand on it, and a sensation came through.

Lana informed Heidi that the name of Loretta's killer was in this binder. She mentioned numbers that appeared in her mind, specifically a page number where the killer's name would be listed. Additionally, she claimed there were pictures of Loretta's killer inside the book as well. The huge binder was never opened during the meeting to test the psychic's premonition; Heidi recalls all Gene Strate could do was look at them in disbelief.

When Lana saw a photograph of Tom Egley much later, Lana told Heidi she knew without a doubt that this was the person who had killed her mother. But a psychic's impressions hold little ground in a court of law. They needed proof, and it didn't help that the county attorney seemed dismissive. Above all, Heidi wanted to bring her mother's killer to justice, and as they left the office that day, her friend turned to her and said, "I know you want justice, Heidi, but you also need to live your life."

It was a humbling statement and a true one. Heidi's desire to find the killer had become an obsession, one driven by the fact that she knew in her gut that Tom was guilty, and the people who could help put him behind bars didn't seem to be helping.

But she couldn't give up. She wouldn't give up. But she was feeling worn down.

That day, as they walked out of the county attorney's office, Lana shared a frightening feeling with her sister, Donna. Heidi was going to die. This dire unease wasn't something she shared with Heidi . . . not until much later, after Heidi barely escaped death.

A broken tooth had caused Heidi's face to begin to swell, and it continued to get worse. Kevin picked her up from the county attorney's office and took her directly to the emergency room. She spent five days in the Price hospital with no definite diagnosis and then was transported to the Provo hospital, where they determined she had a flesh-eating disease called necrotizing fasciitis. She spent fifteen days in the ICU, had five surgeries, three blood transfusions, and flatlined once.

As Heidi teetered on the brink of death, it seemed the clairvoyant's prediction was on the verge of realization. However, in her moments of near unconsciousness, a sensation akin to drowning in darkness, she heard a voice from the void. Somewhere from outside herself, there was a whispering of unresolved earthly matters pertaining to her mother. Startled awake, she fought for breath, clawing her way back from the brink. In a voice strained with separation, she rasped, "What about my mom?"

She remained in the Provo hospital for seventeen days. Heidi's scar, resembling a slit throat, holds a profound significance for her, particularly in relation to her mother's death. The resemblance strikes her as ironic, suggesting a symbolic connection between the physical mark on her body and the traumatic event of her mother's passing.

Each morning, as Heidi faced her reflection in the mirror, the sight of the slit-like scar on her throat served as a poignant reminder of her mother's ultimate sacrifice. This visible symbol of her mother's tragedy fueled Heidi's determination to seek justice for her unsung hero. It was a constant source of strength, propelling her forward in her quest to uncover the truth and honor her mother's memory.

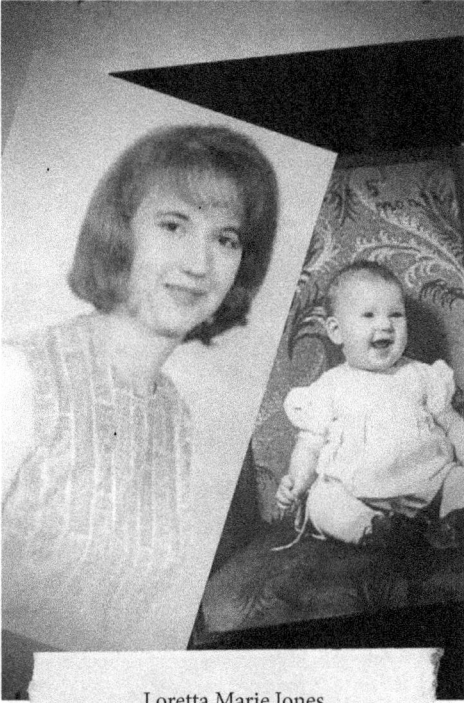
Loretta Marie Jones

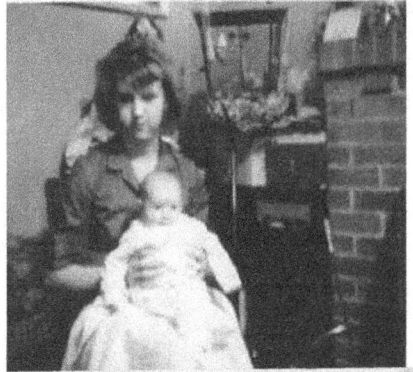
A young Loretta holding her newborn, Heidi

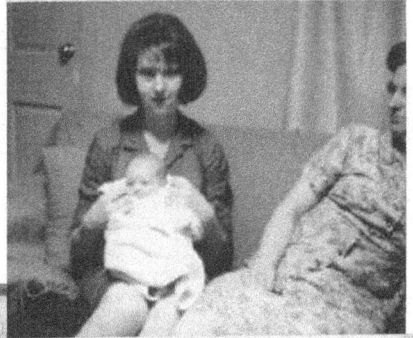
Loretta, Heidi, and LuDeen

Jones Family – 1960s

Heidi – age 4

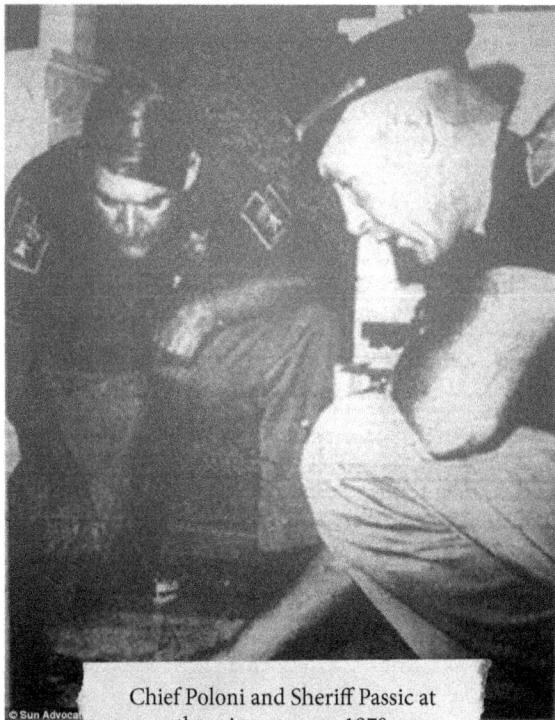
Chief Poloni and Sheriff Passic at the crime scene – 1970

House where Loretta Jones was murdered – 1970

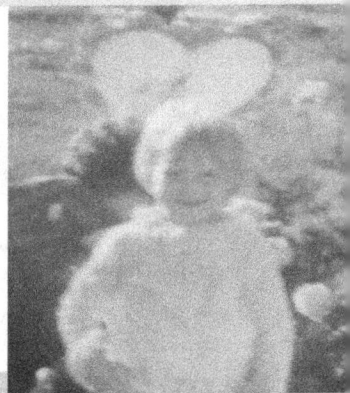
Heidi at her mother's gravesite – 4 years old

Loretta's burial – Elmo City Cemetery, August 1970

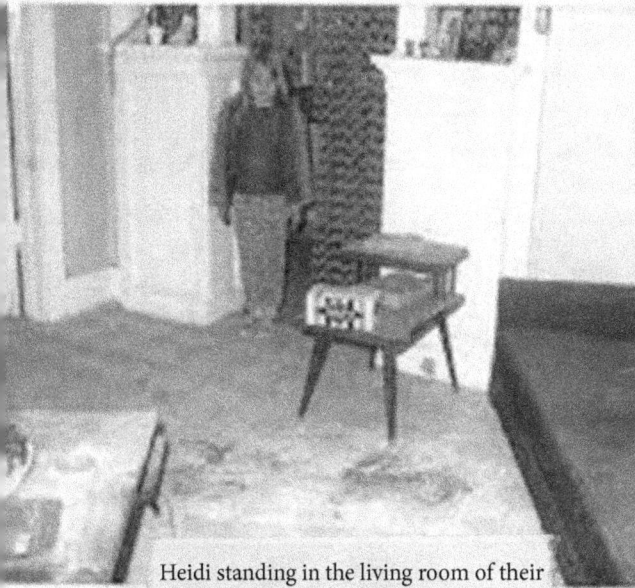
Heidi standing in the living room of their home where the murder took place

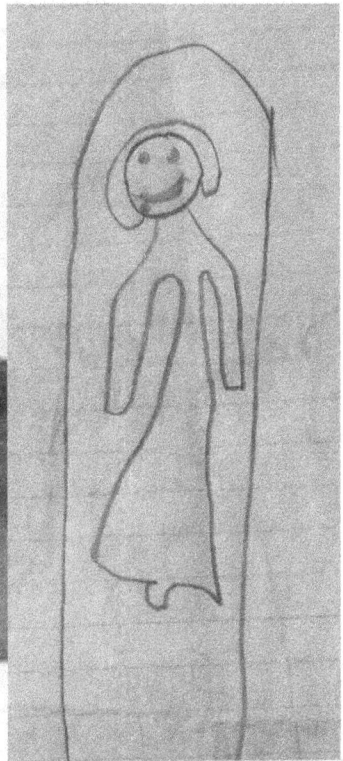
Heidi's drawing of her mother in her casket

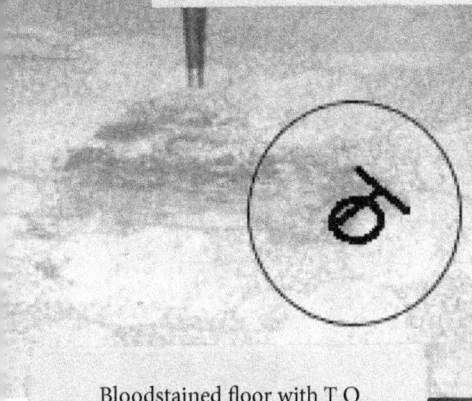
Bloodstained floor with T O

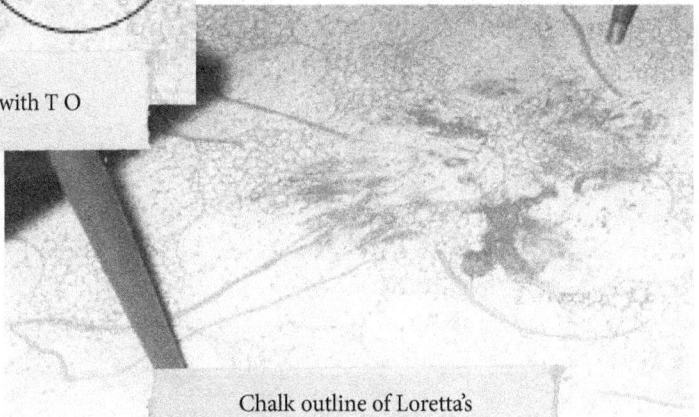
Chalk outline of Loretta's body and bloodstains

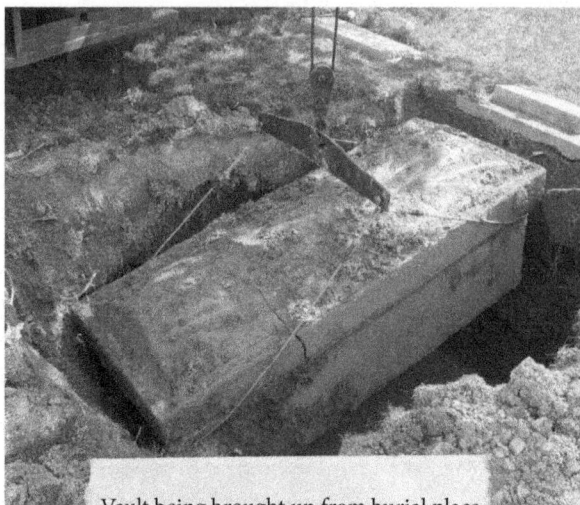
Vault being brought up from burial place

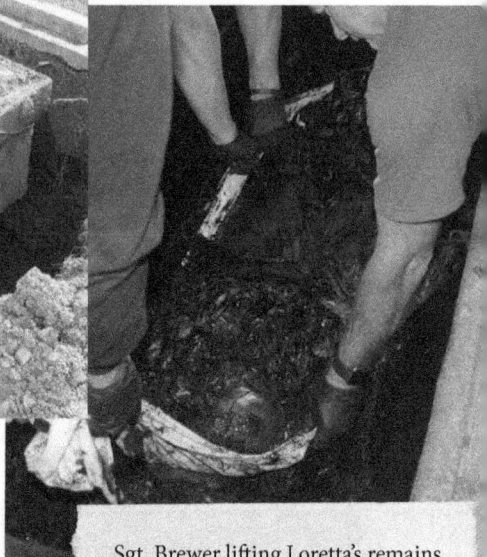
Sgt. Brewer lifting Loretta's remains

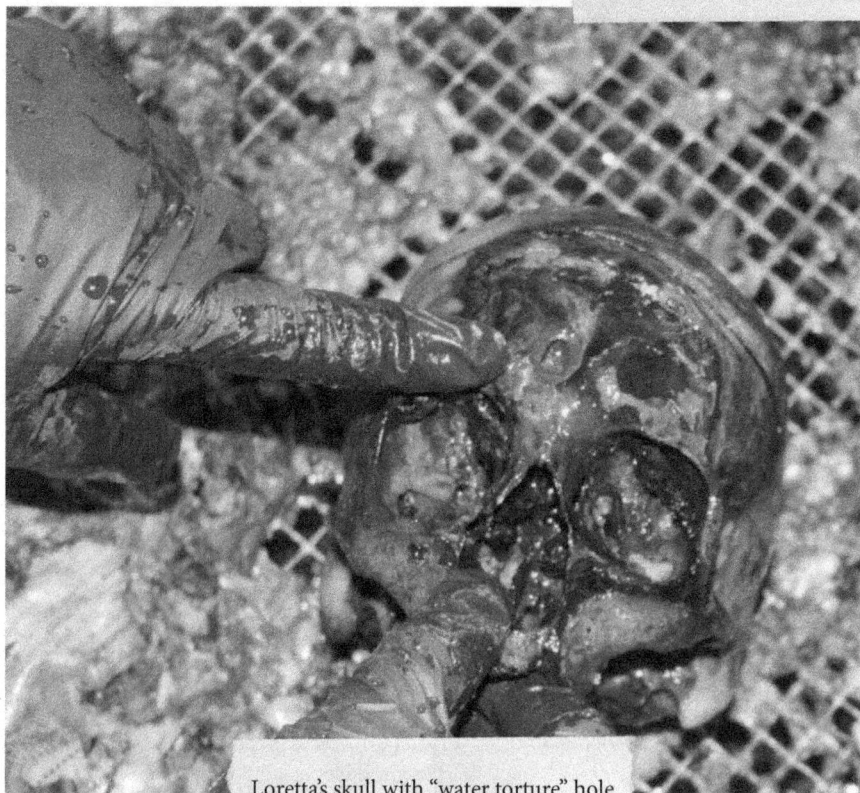
Loretta's skull with "water torture" hole

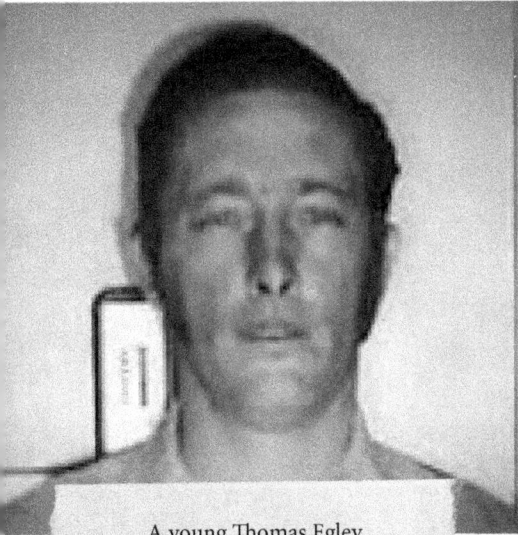

A young Thomas Egley

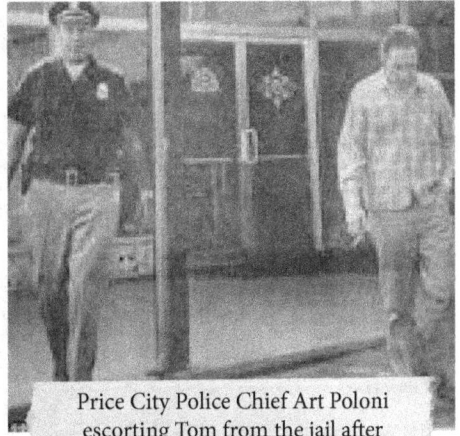

Price City Police Chief Art Poloni escorting Tom from the jail after he was released

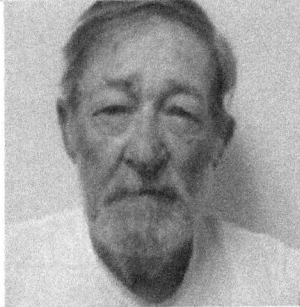

Tom at his sentencing hearing – 2016

An aging Tom Egley

Sgt. David Brewer hugging Heidi the day Egley was convicted

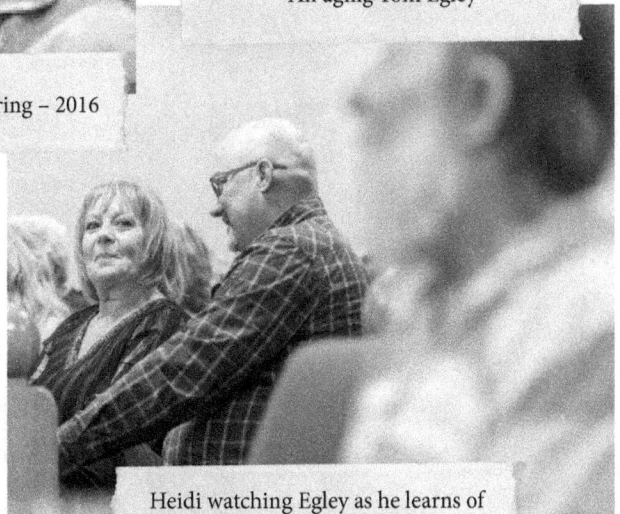

Heidi watching Egley as he learns of his fate (Kevin next to her)

Doll made by Loretta for Heidi

The pink handcuffs presented to Heidi as a gift from Brewer and Walton

Sit pax Have vos

Heidi's Raider's tattoo

Heidi and Kevin at the Justice for Loretta Jones Motorcycle Ride

Sgt Brewer's retirement with Sheriff Jeff Wood (L) and Deputy Sheriff Cletis Steele (R)

At the Paula Zahn taping in New York – Left to right: Jim Kulow, Lori Kulow Fenner, Heidi Jones-Asay, and David Brewer

CHAPTER 21

COUNTY ATTORNEY

During the investigation, Brewer discovered another detail regarding the attack on Lori Kulow, the young girl who had escaped an attempted kidnapping the night of Loretta's murder. After interviewing her and her brother, Sgt. Brewer learned from Kulow that the assailant was wearing an odd multicolored hat, and when he attacked her, the hat fell off. As it turns out, Egley was known to own a welder's cap, one that a witness later reported seeing hanging on a hook outside Egley's door. The hat had been mentioned many times before but was never viewed as being potential evidence.

The case was building up, and yet Brewer could not convince Gene Strate, Carbon County Attorney, to take it to court. When presented with the current state of the evidence, the Utah Attorney General's Office told Sgt. Brewer they might have enough circumstantial evidence to convict Egley. In many cases, criminals can be convicted based on circumstantial evidence, but this leaves wiggle room for the jury to find the suspect innocent.

Tom's own words had confirmed for Brewer that he had murdered Loretta Jones, but it wasn't a confession. Witness statements about the bloody clothes, the laundromat collaboration, statements from Heidi and her family, witness statements from the Kulow case that put Tom in the neighborhood, and the welder's hat added to Brewer's conviction that he was on the right track, but it was all circumstantial evidence. The detective had kept an open mind, but now it was becoming more and more apparent to him that Tom was, without a doubt, guilty, yet the county attorney needed more than Brewer's gut feeling.

What was he missing? He rifled through the bits and pieces of information he had on the 1970 preliminary hearing. Certainly, there had to be a transcript of that court hearing, and perhaps it would render new information to bolster the case. His mission was to track down that record. Brewer had already interviewed everyone he knew to be a part of that long-ago hearing; many were deceased, and most had fuzzy or no recollection of the case at all. Carbon County records indicated that Gayle Cambell had been the court clerk in 1970. It was 2010, and Brewer had learned that she was living in Salt Lake City. He wondered if she would have any information about the missing transcripts, so he reached out to her. Gayle was a pleasant woman who did remember the case, as it had been the first homicide she had done for the court as a stenographer. She remembered the case had been dismissed due to lack of evidence. She also informed him unfortunately, that she had not kept any records from the 1970 court case and only vaguely recalled who testified and why.

Another dead end, Brewer thought.

As a way to get some interest pumped back into the case, Brewer placed an ad in the *Sun Advocate* asking for the public's help in coming forward with any information regarding this case. After the ad ran, a lady called him and said she remembered the curator at the Helper Museum mentioning a black book belonging to Loretta that listed all of her "gentlemen callers," and it was locked up in their safe. Not one to let a stone go unturned, Sgt. Brewer went to the museum.

The Helper Museum offers a fascinating look into Carbon County's coal mining past and the significance of the railroad to the region. From oral histories to themed rooms showcasing artifacts like dinosaur fossils and miniature locomotives, the museum provides a unique glimpse into local history. It features a simulated coal mine, a replica of the company store, and a Veterans Honor Hall, as well as an outdoor exhibit of coal mining equipment.

The first thing Brewer noticed upon his arrival was the distinct smell of coal—earthy, sulfurous, and slightly metallic. It transported him back to his time spent in the Colorado coal mine. Before he could fully explain the reason for the visit, the lady working there took him straight to the back room.

An old safe stood in the dimly lit corner of the antiquated bank vault. Its weathered exterior bore the marks of time, hinting at tales and secrets from bygone eras. The heavy door, now without the security of a lock, suggested a time when security was paramount and trust was tangible.

Brewer peered inside. It was empty. "See, no book. We have never had that book, but we keep hearing rumors about it," she said.

"All part of a modern-day urban legend." Brewer laughed.

Brewer truly believed there was a "black book," which was probably her address book, the place where, like many of us, Loretta kept a list of names, numbers, and addresses. She wrote to many servicemen and had calls from many "boyfriends," etc., so it made sense that she kept a central book to store this information. The term "little black book" is commonly associated with the idea of keeping track of personal and private relationships. Often lovers or romantic interests. Loretta kept a diary for those such musings, so more than likely, it was just an address book.

Brewer believed the original officers took this book into their possession during the initial investigation, and it more than likely ended up being destroyed with the rest of the evidence. He also surmised that if it had names of prominent men listed among its pages, it probably would have been destroyed to get rid of that type of gossip. There was also the fact that Loretta did keep a second diary after her first five-year one ended. Brewer believed it was taken and tossed as well. It would have been interesting to see if Tom's name was mentioned as someone she was dating and what she thought about him.

Lila remembered meeting Tom only once when another couple invited Loretta to double date with them and he picked her up at the house. Loretta let Lila know that she did not care for Tom, and as far as Lila knew, they never went out again.

July 20, 2014, a petition was created on Change.org by Heidi's friend, Twila Martak. Six hundred fifty-seven supporters signed the petition. The petition intended to "Charge and Prosecute in the Murder of Loretta Jones" and was directed at Gene Strate, the county attorney. "Tom Egley needs to be held accountable for the 1970 brutal rape & murder of Loretta Jones. She deserves justice & her family deserves closure. The case was reopened by Carbon County Utah Sheriff's Office in 2010 but has yet to be prosecuted." Many people who signed the petition left comments: "There is still a murderer out there, and he needs to pay for his crime." "Justice for Loretta." "I grew up with her in high school, and her daughter needs closure." The petition yielded no outcome.

After several discouraging meetings with Gene Strate, Sgt. Brewer realized prosecution was not likely from the county office. So he reached out to the Attorney General's Office and set up a meeting with Ed Spann, an investigator from the AG's office and former chief deputy of Uintah County, with over forty years of experience in law enforcement. Sgt. Brewer respected his opinion. "He has a good ear to listen and two cents to give."

Detective Taylor joined Brewer as they traveled to the Salt Lake City office to present the case. The Attorney General's Office expressed interest and offered valuable suggestions. During a subsequent visit, Sheriff James Cordova and Deputy Sheriff Guy Adams accompanied Brewer. On a third visit, Gene Strate joined them, and believe it or not, the AG's office recommended that Strate file the case due to its solid circumstantial evidence, emphasizing they had nothing to lose. The AG's office also pledged to send attorneys to assist with the case. Ed Spann arranged to have photogrammetry (the science and technology of obtaining reliable information about physical objects and the environment through the process of recording, measuring, and interpreting photographic images) done throughout the house where Loretta was murdered. The owners agreed, and a camera was set up in the middle of the room on a tripod and it took 360-degree photos of all the rooms. At the time, this was state-of-the-art stuff. This imaging was done to gain a better insight into the crime scene, document how small it was, and also the view from Heidi's door to the front room. The home had been remodeled, and the old door had been replaced. However, the owners had stored the original door behind the house; the detectives found it and were able to corroborate Heidi's story about seeing her mother's lifeless body through a keyhole. Brewer kept the door at the sheriff's intake building for a long time, not necessarily because it was evidence but because Heidi wanted to keep it, partially for the memory of her mother and partly as motivation to keep the case going even in the face of setbacks. Unfortunately, another deputy mistook the door as trash and took it to the dump.

After the encouragement from the AG's office, Brewer called Strate the next day and asked, "What do you need?" Strate instructed him to make ten copies of everything and get the information to his office. Detectives Taylor and Brewer missed their SWAT training to make the copies and organize them into ten three-ring binders, complete with tab dividers. Each binder was about three inches thick.

The following week, on July 21, 2014 (one day after the petition went to Strate's office), Brewer received a Letter of Declination from the county attorney. "Please be advised that this office is declining prosecution on this matter. It has been many months since our meeting with the attorney general prosecutors in Salt Lake City. The consensus at that time was that there was insufficient evidence to charge Egley." Brewer was shocked. Stunned. Outraged. Had they not both attended the same meeting with the AG's office, where they actively encouraged the county attorney to move forward and even offered assistance with the case? It was a sucker punch from left field.

Brewer then learned that Mr. Strate had met with the Jones family prior to mailing the declination letter without Brewer's or Heidi's knowledge, and Strate said they had told him not to prosecute. LuDeen told Brewer at a follow-up meeting that this was not true. LuDeen also shared that Strate had not informed the family that the AG's office had felt they had enough circumstantial evidence to try the case.

But Brewer did not give up on trying to convince the county attorney there was enough to push the case forward. After the seminar, when the exhumation idea was introduced, he set up another meeting with Gene Strate and his deputy county attorney, Jeremy Humes. He introduced his desire to exhume the body of Loretta Jones. "Why?" was the response he received from the senior attorney. Brewer explained the possibility of DNA and was met with the question, "What makes you think there is DNA?" He was dismayed by this question because, over and over in the reports, it mentioned that sperm had been present and swabs had been taken and sent in for lab analysis.

As he left their office, Gene Strate offhandedly offered him good luck and then added, "Oh, and by the way, some lady dropped off the preliminary hearing."

What? Brewer was astonished. After taking a moment to register this information, he asked Strate if he had read the report and what his opinion had been. Strate had reviewed the transcript and offered that it mostly contained a bunch of lawyers arguing back and forth.

"When did she drop it off?" Brewer asked.

Back in December.

It was now April 2016.

CHAPTER 22

PRELIMINARY REPORT

S gt. Brewer devoured the report, hoping for new information that would direct him forward. What he learned, however, was not so much new information as confirmation
that he was on the right track. From the beginning, on his own,
he had been able to reconstruct the case pretty close, right up to
the 1970 preliminary hearing.

The preliminary hearing is like a mini trial. The prosecution
will call witnesses and introduce evidence, and the defense can
cross-examine witnesses. However, the defense cannot object to
using certain evidence, and in fact, evidence that could not be
shown to a jury at trial is allowed to be presented at a preliminary hearing.

Sgt. Brewer took pride in having no files at his disposal when
this unusual case landed in his lap. He felt that the initial police
investigation might have biased the direction he took in solving
the murder, and for him, a blank slate was the best place to begin. Sure, it would have been nice to have an old case file to refer

to, but in his mind, the investigation had been unsuccessful in producing a conviction, so almost everything in the file would be useless. He was glad he had nothing to cloud his judgment and could start with an open mind. So from the beginning, he began putting the dusty puzzle together step by step without any preconceived ideas. If a piece didn't fit, he'd try another until the edges of the worn-out part were twisted and turned, persistently adjusting until they finally nestled into the place where they belonged. Solving the puzzle became an addictive pursuit, and when all the pieces fell into place, the complete picture of justice started to emerge.

He had done his share of interviewing those who were still alive and had witnessed, testified, or been involved in the case back in the 1970s, but if he could glean one new clue from this report that would spin the compass in the right direction, he would be relieved.

He methodically went through the report, from the swearing-in of the official district court reporter to the instructions on how she should file the transcripts with the clerk of the district court. The players were the Honorable Tom G. Platis, Dan C. Keller, and Boyd Bunnell, attorneys for the plaintiff, and Thorit Hatch, defense attorney.

The state called their first witness, Sue Ann Horvath, the neighbor who was first to find Loretta's body after Heidi had informed her son Lance that she thought her mother was dead. There was nothing new within her testimony.

Parley D. Jones was put on the stand next. He offered that he witnessed lights being on in Loretta's house around 9:45 p.m. and that the house was dark around 10:05 p.m. Parley's construction yard was across the street from Loretta's house, and he had been there gathering materials for his next job with his son Duane Jones. His statements corroborated other testimony Brewer had gathered.

Next was Arther Poloni, Price City police chief. He was called to the scene by Sue Ann Horvath, and when he arrived, he found the victim "lying with her head south, face down, right next to a coffee table." Other officers started to arrive, including Officer McCourt, Sheriff Passic, Officer Tildon (sic), Officer Vuksinick, and Officer Bryner.

This was the first time Sgt. Brewer had heard the names of other officers at the scene and found this new information to be very helpful. Brewer would later interview Officer Bryner, who confirmed a compelling story.

Chief Poloni stated he called for a county attorney and Dr. Robinson to come to the scene. He asked Sheriff Passic to take photographs, which were labeled and stored in the Carbon County Sheriff's Office safe. At this point, the court took the time to view and discuss the details of each photo, and they were entered as Exhibits 1–7.

One photo was of Loretta's panties, and the description from Poloni caught Brewer's attention. "We didn't touch them. We looked, and it appeared they had been cut with a knife or some sharp instrument." Brewer had always thought the panties had just been pulled down along with the "shorts" the police had identified in an earlier photograph. And although this wasn't a "clue" as to who did it, Brewer thought of it more of a clue as to the character of the person who did it. It said that Loretta had not agreed to sex and so the perpetrator had to cut the thin material so he could rape her.

Brewer had always wondered when the rape had occurred the night of the murder. Had Egley raped her and then killed her to silence her? Or had he stabbed her first to gain control over a struggling victim and then raped her?

The rug Loretta had been lying on when they arrived was discussed, and Poloni explained how it had been bagged and tagged for evidence. It was also placed in the safe at the sheriff's office and subsequently sent to the FBI, along with twenty-eight other items to be analyzed.

Loretta's house was described as being "orderly and clean." The bed was made, and the front door was open, but the back door was locked with a bolt-type lock. Everything in the kitchen had been washed and sitting in a drainer. The garbage was in a garbage pail on the back porch. Nothing was mentioned about a forced entry or a struggle inside the house.

These details were useful for Brewer, who would later link them with his theory about Egley buying hamburgers and sharing them with Loretta.

When asked about the couch and the bloodstain observed in the photographs, Poloni was asked to describe what he observed regarding these. "There were some bloodstains on the floor. A lot of blood from the victim. Lots of blood on the back of her blouse. Her hair was matted with blood. Up near the right hand, there were some bloodstains and also some blood smears on the floor. Up by her right hand, looked like her right hand had moved back and forth on the floor. There was also blood on her arm and one bloodstain on her buttocks. A lot of blood on her back and matted in the back of her hair. Blood coming out of her nose."

Brewer later learned more about these smears in a fascinating tale and added these critical details to the big puzzle.

The attorneys moved on to questioning Poloni about his August 1 interview with Tom Egley. He advised the court he had read Tom the Miranda Warning, and Tom had stated he did not want an attorney at that time. Then Poloni went on to share what Egley had told him. Tom had known Loretta for about a year but hadn't seen her for approximately two months. Tom stated he had not been to her house on July 30 and had thumbed a ride to Price with the Kirkwood boys. They stopped at the Highway Rendezvous (a bar in Spring Glen midway between Price and Helper), had a beer, and then he had them drop him off by the Arctic Circle in Price, where he ordered a couple of hamburgers, walked down the street, and sat on the curb and ate them. Tom told Poloni he then walked uptown and did a little window-shopping for a couple of hours. He then hitched a ride with two boys from Kenilworth, who dropped him off at the Kenilworth crossing, and from there he walked to the Highway Rendezvous. He stated he was "feeling pretty good." Inside the bar he asked a couple of guys for a ride back to Helper, and after a beer, Fritz Martinez gave him a ride to Helper, and he went up to his room and went to bed. Tom told Poloni he arrived in Price that night around 9:00 p.m. and was back home about 11:30–11:45 p.m.

The state's attorney, Mr. Keller, confirmed that the Arctic Circle on 400 East and Main was approximately four and a half blocks from Loretta's home.

Brewer wondered if law enforcement had the mind to obtain receipts from the Arctic Circle or interview an employee who could verify Tom's claim. The time of the purchase and what he purchased (how many burgers) would have been good evidence for the case.

Now knowing some of the locations, Brewer obtained aerial maps from the county, which showed the proximity of the Arctic Circle to Loretta's house. On that same block were the apartments where Lori Kulow lived during the attempted abduction. Sgt. Brewer was able to track Egley's steps on the night of the murder on this aerial map. It confirmed that across the street from the Newhouse Hotel was the laundromat where Egley supposedly went to wash his clothes, and right next to that building was a small circle on the map, which could have been the burn barrel mentioned by Barbara Busio in her earlier statement. As a side note from Brewer, he found it odd that Egley would have gone to the laundromat alone, as that wasn't something men did in the seventies, and he asked around and learned that burn barrels were used in the days when most people had coal furnaces. They used these barrels to discard their clinkers (burned-down coal chunks).

The defense then questioned Police Chief Poloni, and Mr. Hatch, starting with the blood in the room and on Loretta's body, asked, "Did you examine the body for wounds?"

Poloni explained that after the sheriff, the county attorney, and Dr. Robinson had arrived, together they identified what appeared to be stab wounds in the back, approximately fourteen. "We turned the body over, and there were two in the chest and one in the throat."

"Was there any evidence of any kind that the victim had put up any kind of struggle?"

"No, sir, there was not."

"Were there any cut marks on her hands?"

"Not to my knowledge, there were not."

Jumping ahead to the later testimony of the Utah state medical examiner, Edward F. Wilson, who under oath answered the question, "There weren't any scratches or abrasions on the hands as if maybe they had been caused by protecting herself?" with "There was one on the wrist." He further answered, "Yes, sir," to the follow-up of, "It's compatible with the facts that they could be defense wounds, is that right?"

For Brewer, this new fact made sense. It is rare that a victim would not try to fight off an assailant as they were attacked with a knife, coming away without defense wounds. It's a natural reaction.

One last redirect came from Mr. Keller, who returned to the subject of the one spot of blood that had been documented between the body and the front door. When asked to describe the blood spot, Poloni said, "It looked to be as if someone had stepped in some blood and that it was a partial shoe print."

That was also interesting to Brewer. Had this clue been followed up on?

Sheriff Albert Passic took the stand and testified it had been his job, as requested by the police chief, to photograph the victim's residence and body. His testimony closely correlated with what Poloni had already told the court.

A few additional details emerged when Passic described his interview with Tom Egley. Passic told the court that "I went back to the point [when he was interviewing Tom] and asked him [Tom] if he had an encounter with a little girl, and he said no, that he didn't have an encounter with a little girl."

One new fact that came out of the preliminary hearing for Brewer was that Egley had called Loretta the night of the murder. Sheriff Passic testified that in a conversation with Tom, when asked when he called Loretta and what they talked about, the transcripts noted, "He said he called her that night on the phone and said that he just talked about generalities. He said nothing specific. In fact, he said he called her to ask her how she was." Phone records?

Next, Passic said he questioned Tom about taking a lie detector test. Tom told Passic no, he didn't think he would take one at that time. When Poloni tried to impress upon him that they were trying to prove his innocence as well as guilt, Tom said, "He thought it was our job to find him guilty, that he didn't think he had to prove himself innocent."

Tom confirmed that he was "wearing a funny hat" at the time, and Poloni learned that the hat was in his room in Helper. He told the officer he could have the hat, but then Tom added, "Look, I'm getting too involved in this situation. I want to call my attorney." With that, he was allowed to use the phone.

Tom did agree to having his blood drawn and gave them hair samples. The officers drove to Helper and secured the hat. While in his room, they saw lying on the dresser an old-timer's knife, which Passic stated he asked if he could have. Tom said, "Yes," then added, "I have a couple more here if you want to take those too." Passic asked for the clothes Tom wore on the night of July 30, and Tom went to his drawer and took out a pair of Levi's and a T-shirt. The sheriff described the clothes as being folded and appeared to have been laundered. He testified that he had obtained a pair of Tom's canvas tennis shoes later, and both the shoes and the hat appeared to be "just washed or cleaned."

Passic listed for the court items that had been sent to the FBI.

From Tom: Three knives, a pair of trousers, a T-shirt, tennis shoes, and a hat. His blood, hair, and pubic hair samples were also included.

From Loretta: Hairs from her brassiere, left- and right-hand fingernail clippings, a Band-Aid, and "material that was on the left side of her body, some dirt." The dirt was explained to be "debris from the body and sheet." Pubic hair, eyelashes, eyebrow hair, scalp hair, and blood samples were also sent.

Other samples were from the rug, pillow, blouse, brassiere, shorts, panties, and couch cover.

At this point, the court reminded Mr. Hatch it was almost noon, and the judge recessed until two p.m.

CHAPTER 23

After Recess

W ith all parties fed and refreshed, they picked up the case and discussed how the items were labeled, packaged, and sent to the FBI before hearing testimony from the next witness, Edward F. Wilson, the state medical examiner whose impressive credentials were noted for the court. He received his medical degree from Yale and completed his residency at Johns Hopkins Hospital.

He was first asked to explain his initial autopsy findings, which covered the basic information, weight, height, sex, etc. of the victim.

His testimony then went into the particulars of the wounds that he had identified, first those on Loretta's back (he found sixteen) and then on to her neck and chest. When asked if he had an opinion as to the cause of death, he stated, "Yes. The cause of death was due to internal bleeding due to stab wounds in the pulmonary artery, lungs, and heart." He later testified that he felt that the abrasion on the neck, the blood beneath the skin, and the little spots in the eyes and airway were consistent with asphyxia. They would be brought on by an obstruction to breathing or by an obstruction to the blood vessels in the neck, as by grabbing somebody by the throat, he added.

Brewer and others always thought the cause of Loretta's death was a slash to the throat. Yes, the neck appeared to have a stab wound, but the doctor was sharing his opinion that Loretta had been strangled.

Dr. Wilson was asked if he could tell whether or not, at the time of the stab wound inflictions, the victim was alive or dead. The doctor's answer was, "The person was alive at that time." He then went on to answer the question, "How long could someone live with stab wounds like that?" He said it would not be an hour or immediately, but more in terms of minutes. He also added in his professional opinion that it was possible for a person to be rendered unconscious by strangulation and still be alive.

He confirmed for Brewer that, from an examination of the vaginal contents, there had been sperm present. The next question was one that Brewer had not considered: "Would it be possible to tell whether this sperm was placed there while the person was dead or alive?" The doctor answered, "I could not tell that."

According to Utah Code Section 76-9-704—Abuse or desecration of a dead human body as described in Subsections (2) (b) through (e) is a third-degree felony. Had the ME been able to make that determination, it is possible that an additional charge could have been added to Egley's crimes. Had he raped Loretta before or after her death? Or, even more horrifying, while she was dying?

The ME confirmed the contents of Loretta's stomach ("unidentifiable brown material, potatoes, cheese, [vegetable] skins, tomatoes, onion, and lettuce") and added that it usually takes the stomach four to six hours to empty once the food is taken in.

Brewer reflected back to how many times witnesses and Tom himself had mentioned that he had purchased burgers at the nearby Arctic Circle. Poloni's statement indicated that the kitchen was clean and garbage had been taken to the back porch. In Brewer's mind, this evidence contradicted the idea that Tom had bought burgers to be eaten by him and Loretta at her house. Poloni testified that Tom had bought a couple of burgers for himself and ate them on the curb. Brewer believed this was where Tom formulated his plan to snatch Lori Kulow. He doubted that Tom would have bought enough burgers to share with Loretta and Heidi and held on to them during an attempted kidnapping. It would have been easy for law enforcement to obtain the receipts from Arctic Circle and interview employees regarding the time, date, and details of Tom's purchase. Had this been done?

Brewer conjured up a scenario and played it through his mind. What if, after Tom's thwarted kidnapping attempt, he went back to the burger place and purchased more hamburgers in an attempt to gain entry into Loretta's home by arriving with dinner? Poloni's statement regarding the clean and orderly condition of Loretta's kitchen didn't match this possibility. It doesn't seem like Loretta would have sat down with someone she didn't want in her home to eat a burger and then clean up before she was attacked. Remember, Tom said he bought a couple of burgers and ate them before walking around the area, window-shopping. He had not shown up at Loretta's with dinner even though he told his girlfriend, Marsha, that he had. The evidence in the kitchen did not support this.

So what about the ME's report that Loretta had "burger-like" contents in her stomach? Burgers are a popular meal. Perhaps she and Heidi had gone out earlier for lunch, or they might have shared a casserole made from the same ingredients: meat, potatoes, cheese, tomatoes, onion, and lettuce. What about tacos and tater tots? To Brewer, it seemed like more of a coincidence.

The last question to Dr. Wilson was a challenge from Mr. Hatch regarding his testimony that the abrasions on Loretta were caused by strangulation: "But you don't know what caused this abrasion on the neck or the bleeding inside, do you?"

"Well, it's just my opinion."

"But you don't know what it is; it could have been many things, couldn't it?"

"Yes, sir."

"You are excused, Doctor. Thank you."

CHAPTER 24

PAGES 59—90

On a quiet Saturday morning, Brewer sat at his kitchen table, bleary-eyed and tired, surrounded by the lingering aroma of freshly brewed coffee. With a weary sigh, he flipped through the fifty-eight pages of the ninety-page preliminary report, his mind racing as missing pieces slowly fell into place. Despite the fatigue weighing heavily on him, Brewer felt a surge of adrenaline as the report unveiled new leads and presented compelling arguments. Each sip of coffee fueled his determination to uncover the truth behind the case he had devoted countless hours to solving.

With caffeine racing through his body and sunshine calling his name, Brewer needed to put the report aside and do something for himself. A little exercise and fresh air would do him good. Many years ago, he had purchased a metal detector, and more often than he wished, it sat propped up in the corner of his garage. Today, adventure called. In previous detecting trips, he learned that Carbon County was rich with "treasures." Over centuries, coal miners, railroad workers, and immigrants had left traces of their journeys, scattering lost items along the way. His most valued find was an 1878 twenty-dollar gold coin, which he coincidently found a hundred feet from where Tom Egley had lived at the Newhouse Hotel in Helper. "People joke that was my payment for solving the case." Brewer chuckled. "If Tom had thrown his knife in the river like he said he did, he would have walked over the top of this gold coin without even knowing it." Although he didn't always find anything of value, Brewer enjoyed hiking around exploring. Mindless and free.

Today's finds included a tarnished ring, some bottle caps, and a few coins. Yet, despite his efforts, he struggled to stay focused as he swept the metal detector back and forth over the hard ground. As he walked a few feet, his mind wandered back to the last pages of the preliminary report, the case perpetually consuming his thoughts.

Charles Kirkwood, age sixteen, took the stand in the case of the State of Utah against Tom Egley on the afternoon of November 5, 1970. He verified that he and his brother had given Tom a ride to Price the night of July 30, 1970. They picked him up in Helper around eight thirty p.m. and dropped him at the Conoco, a gas station in Price across from the Arctic Circle on Main Street, where Tom said he wanted to buy some cigarettes. They made a halfway stop at the Highway Rendezvous bar in Spring Glen for about ten minutes. Then Charles gave different testimony from an earlier statement he had written at the Helper Police Department. His prior statement said, "We took Tom Egley to Price, and then he said he was going to get some cigarettes and go see his girl." Now Charles was saying he "wasn't sure about 'that last part' [the girl part] of his statement." After being asked to verify that it was indeed his signature on that earlier statement, Charles added, "Well, I was sure then, but now I'm not too sure now." He added that he had started to think about it and said he had not been coerced or threatened by anyone to change his statement. Keller reminded him of their meeting the night before, where he was asked about this statement. Mr. Kirkwood said he remembered saying that to Mr. Keller but added, "And that is when I started thinking about it." There were a few objections, but the statement was left hanging without resolve.

Charles's testimony ended with him describing the hat Egley was wearing—"He had a polka-dotted hat on"—and his boots—"railroad boots with rounded toes." Brewer wondered if these boots would have matched the bloody shoe prints noted by the investigators at the scene of the crime. Or if anyone even tried.

Margaret Hamilton, owner of the Highway Rendezvous bar, testified next. Yes, she had seen Tom when he and the Kirkwood boys came in around five p.m. for a few minutes. She also saw him later that same evening between eleven and eleven thirty p.m. Tom was alone and told her he had walked from Price and now needed a ride the rest of the way to Helper. She said something along the lines of, "You walked this far; just walk right back." She said Tom and Fritz Martinez had a conversation about Fritz giving him a ride but that Fritz left before Tom did.

Other detailed recollections from Hamilton included Tom ordering a glass of beer but never drinking it. He appeared nervous and went to the door several times, looking up and down the road. "He had on a little cap that was, well, I call it a crazy cap." She described the hat as being of all colors. She recalled that his clothes were dirty and he had spots all over the T-shirt. "It [his T-shirt] was all spotted. It looked like it was red."

At this point, all the witnesses had been called, and from pages 76–85 in the preliminary report, Attorney Bunnell made some judicial arguments, followed by Mr. Hatch informing the judge that the defendant wanted to make a statement under oath.

The report states: "TOM EGLEY, the defendant in this action, stands and makes the following unsworn statement:

"I would like to say that I didn't kill the girl, and I wasn't down there that night. And as far as telling the Kirkwood boys that I was going to see a girl, I didn't say that. I just had them stop so that I could get me some cigarettes. That's it, Your Honor."

Brewer wondered why Tom was allowed to give this statement without being sworn in and also felt his statement was contrary to the direct testimony they had just heard. All the witnesses stated he had been in Price the night of July 30, and now he was denying it. Egley's concern for the Kirkwood statement was such an odd thing to defend when much more was being accused of him.

The court recessed at four thirty p.m.

The next day, November 6, 1970, at 11:50 a.m., a decision was returned.

Those in attendance stood and awaited the judge's decision. Had the state put forth enough evidence that the judge felt compelled to hold the case over for trial? Had Loretta's killer finally been identified?

"The Court, in view of the evidence given in the Preliminary Hearing finds that there is not sufficient cause to believe the Defendant guilty of the public offense charged."

Tom Egley was ordered discharged, and the court instructed the reporter to transcribe the court notes into longhand and file them with the clerk of the district court.

Brewer had the foresight to know how the hearing concluded; however, it still felt unjust, and it brought up questions that would never be answered, but he asked them to himself anyway. Why hadn't Marsha testified about Tom's behavior and clothes? Her input would have been helpful for the state's case.

And as far as Charles Kirkwood being Tom's alibi. Brewer felt his testimony only confirmed that he had given Tom a ride and dropped him off in Price. The timeline fit with the timeline of the murder, and his location of being four blocks from Loretta's put him near the scene of the crime. This was coupled with the earlier phone call to Loretta and the attempted kidnapping of Lori Kulow.

All these little bits and pieces, Brewer felt, added up to a lot of circumstantial evidence that made him believe, even more than before, that Tom Egley had murdered Loretta Jones the night of July 30, 1970.

CHAPTER 25

TRUE LOVE

Have you ever met someone and found yourself going from breakfast to bowling and ending with a movie all in one unforgettable day? That was how Heidi and Kevin spent their first date together, a perpetual day that would continue from 2012 until they were married in 2015.

Kevin and Heidi were already friends on Facebook; after all, Kevin had grown up as one of her brother Bryon's friends. They kept in touch throughout the years, but it wasn't until Kevin's divorce was final in 2012 that they took their relationship down a different path. Kevin started making the long 140-mile trip to Grantsville, where Heidi was living with her sister Lila, from his home in Helper. Heidi, in an effort to help with the commute, started spending more and more time in Helper. So much so that Lila finally claimed her guest bedroom back and helped Heidi move in with Kevin. They shared a cozy home on Helper's quaint Main Street. A place that looked like time had moved on without it.

LuDeen liked Kevin. She shared everyone's opinion of the easygoing, sweet-loving man that her granddaughter was in love with. It was a bittersweet realization that LuDeen, having passed away in May, would not be present at Heidi's wedding in June of the same year.

As the wedding day approached for the first-time bride, Heidi found herself navigating a whirlwind of emotions. Amid the excitement and anticipation of her impending marriage, there lingered a profound sense of loss and sorrow. The recent passing of her grandmother, who had raised her, cast a shadow over the joyous occasion. Their relationship had been complex, marked by both love and discord. While she mourned the absence of her grandmother, there was also a bittersweet acknowledgment of the new chapter in her life about to unfold. As she walked down the aisle, she carried with her a blend of grief and hope, honoring the memory of her grandmother while embracing the promise of her future. Heidi found LuDeen's death particularly difficult, feeling as though she had lost another mother. Despite their significant role adjustments, neither Heidi nor LuDeen made a fuss when Heidi moved in with her grandparents after Loretta's passing. LuDeen seamlessly transitioned from babysitter and grandmother to mother. Heidi grew up alongside her new siblings, adjusting without complications, and she acknowledged that LuDeen did her best in her caretaking role. However, LuDeen's death prompted another round of grieving for Heidi, and she mourned the loss of someone so dear to her. But she knew LuDeen would be happy about her marriage to Kevin.

Heidi wore a charming white summer dress complemented by a blue denim vest and a pearl necklace that had belonged to her mother. An old handkerchief that had been LuDeen's was tucked in a pocket. She had fulfilled all four requirements from the classic saying "something old, something new, something borrowed, something blue." Kevin, reminiscent of a dashing Jim Belushi, sported a crisp white button-down shirt paired with jeans. Complete with a Blues Brothers–inspired hat and bolo tie, they radiated as a striking couple. Heidi clutched a bouquet of vibrant sunflowers and gracefully walked down the aisle, flanked by Lynn and Rick, the husbands of Carolyn and Lila.

Many of Heidi's family and friends traveled the distance to Lake Tahoe, Nevada, to witness her wedding. But as the vows were exchanged, a poignant emptiness marked the spot where Loretta's presence was sorely missed. Heidi always felt Loretta's guiding spirit, a bond they shared throughout their lives. Yet the tangible moments were irreplaceable: the comforting touch of a mother fussing over her hair, ensuring the bouquet was just so, and sharing in the tears of happiness. Heidi deeply felt Loretta's presence and absence, a mix of joy for the moment and a profound sense of loss for a lifetime.

The couple had been renting a duplex on Helper's Main Street, but once they tied the knot, they purchased a completely remodeled four-bedroom, two-bath home built in the forties. The detached garage was what sold it to Kevin, and they committed to making Helper their hometown.

Heidi often did business in Helper's downtown, which took her by the Newhouse Hotel where Tom Egley lived in 1970. The once stately building had fallen into such disrepair that its dilapidated facade looked creepy and foreboding. The hotel was now owned by a "weird self-proclaimed artist" whose name Heidi couldn't remember. She would often see him sitting out front. When a For Sale sign went up, Heidi asked if she could look inside. His excuse for not permitting her to enter was that it was too dirty. After it was sold, the new owner held a yard sale and let Heidi enter, but only into the first floor for safety reasons.

The renovation has breathed new life into the old building, giving it a much-needed facelift. The owners have ambitious plans for the vintage structure, envisioning a multifunctional space that caters to various interests and activities. Among their plans are to transform it into an event space complete with a saloon, an art gallery, a workshop and retreat area, a gift shop, and even a tea parlor. Additionally, the upper floors will be converted into comfortable residential apartments.

Once complete, this eclectic venue will serve as a hub for both locals and tourists alike, offering a unique gathering place in the artsy town. It's expected to attract many visitors, particularly during events such as the annual Helper Art Festival, the one where Heidi had reconnected with her high school classmate, David Brewer. Helper's Main Street balances itself with old and new. A historic icon, standing proud since 1960, is the eighteen-foot fiberglass statue of a coal miner named Big John, an unofficial memorial to the many minors who lost their lives since mining started in the area in the 1890s.

One of the many interests Kevin shared with Heidi was motorcycles. "He started with a Yamaha and now is on his fourth Harley Davidson," Heidi said with pride. It was Kevin who arranged the "Justice for Loretta Jones Ride" in 2016. The group started at the Price ballpark and drove by the house Loretta had been murdered in, up, over, and back Fairview Canyon to meet at the Elmo Cemetery, where a candlelight vigil was held. The ride was featured in an ETV news article "46 Years Later: Tribute

Ride Held for Loretta Jones," published August 2, 2016—Chantz Richens. The ride was also documented on the "Justice For Loretta Jones" Facebook page.

Behind the scenes, since their first date back in 2012, Kevin has been a constant pillar of support for Heidi, always ready to listen and offer his unwavering support.

CHAPTER 26

THE EXHUMATION

Y ou ready?" Sgt. David Brewer turned to face Heidi, beads
of sweat forming across his forehead. Even beneath the
shade of the trees, the cemetery radiated warmth. Maybe it
was the sun bouncing off the concrete headstones or the tension
in the air as they waited on the precipice of things to come.

Heidi was ready. She'd been ready long before this. Confidence had replaced trepidation. Over time, Heidi had undergone a remarkable transformation, evolving from the
timid and fearful child who once struggled to comprehend
the weight of the word *murder*. Through her journey of seeking justice for her mother, she gradually found her voice and
inner strength. With each new revelation and obstacle over-
come, Heidi gained a deeper understanding of herself and the
world around her. She learned to confront her fears head-on,
no longer allowing them to hold her back. Through perseverance and determination, Heidi emerged as a resilient and
empowered individual, ready to face whatever challenges lay
ahead with courage and conviction.

Heidi had always wondered if DNA could be used to solve her mother's murder, and she first brought up the idea of exhumation in 2009 to her grandmother, LuDeen. LuDeen adamantly objected and refused to stand for it. Not on any religious grounds, but it was just something that wasn't done. "No" was always her firm answer. Years passed, and in 2015, LuDeen was buried next to her husband, Parley, and their daughter Loretta in the same Elmo cemetery where Heidi now stood.

On June 8, 2016, as a group gathered at the exhumation site, emotions ran high, and a mix of sorrow, anticipation, and lingering disbelief was noticeable among those present. It was a rare and curious occurrence, adding to the gravity of the moment and the weight of unresolved questions hanging in the air. The body of twenty-three-year-old Loretta Jones had rested peacefully in this small cemetery since 1970, and today's events hoped to expose her killer's identity. She had been buried for forty-six years, and fingers were crossed that enough soft tissue would be left on the corpse to extract DNA.

Heidi's husband, Kevin, stood by her side, gripping her hand. Sgt. Brewer wiped his forehead, ready for what they might find. And beside them stood Dr. Rachel Walton, who, even before the coffin had been brought up, had looked over the lay of the land and saw the surrounding hayfields. Water could be an issue.

It was a beautiful summer day. Hot, sunny, a cloudless sky stretching to the horizon. Heidi and David gave the okay to start, and the small crowd collectively held their breath. With LuDeen's passing, Heidi was now able to approve the exhumation and signed the required form. The sheriff's office had coordinated with Elmo City to arrange for a backhoe operator and a flatbed truck. The town of Elmo had just purchased a new backhoe, one they'd offered up for the exhumation. All eyes followed the large, noisy piece of machinery as it crept across the manicured lawn and rumbled toward the grave; gears ground and squealed as the shovel lifted into the air, and the pungent odor of diesel fumes wafted upward. Raising its head as high as possible to gain momentum, the large arm swiftly swung down, hit the soil . . . and stopped. The motor stopped. The motion stopped. Even the air seemed to halt with a sense of nothingness.

After a few moments of unanimated suspense, the workers attempted to get the backhoe started again. It made no sense that a new piece of equipment would abruptly stop working. To compound the confusion, the cloudless sky that had allowed the sun's heat to perspire the group turned a dark gray, and a sudden storm violently swept over the cemetery. Wild, tumultuous wind tore leaves off trees and ripped off branches. The group clung to their hats and each other. Police tape that had cordoned off the designated graveyard area stretched and snapped in the chaos.

Heidi looked down at the grave beside her mother's and knew without a doubt it was LuDeen's voice that raged in the wind. She was exercising one last act of control from the grave. "Speak your piece, LuDeen," Heidi whispered to her. And then let it rest.

And just as abruptly as the storm started, it ceased with a sudden and dramatic finality, leaving behind an eerie stillness in its wake. Roaring one minute and silent clear skies the next. And if that wasn't strange enough, the backhoe miraculously roared to life. Everyone agreed they had witnessed something very unusual. Even Sgt. Brewer couldn't deny the weird series of events and had no scientific explanation to offer. He nodded for the workers to repeat the steps of bringing the shovel up and down. It repeated this robotic motion until its clawlike arm struck something beneath the soil.

The workers jumped into the newly dug hole to measure the distance remaining before the backhoe would contact the concrete vault holding Loretta Jones's coffin. A few more feet should do it—two, actually. But instead of hitting the vault, something else happened. The dry soil bubbled beneath the shovel, and the dirt turned to mud. Not a good sign.

The sentiments of those present at the gravesite immediately went from hopeful to uncertain. If water was in the grave, would there be water in the vault?

The possibility of finding DNA on a body depends on various factors, mainly the preservation conditions. Under ideal conditions, like a cool and dry environment, DNA can potentially survive for long periods. The molecule of life has a lifespan of its own. A study of DNA extracted from the leg bones of extinct moa birds in New Zealand found that the half-life of DNA is 521 years. However, DNA degradation can occur over time due to various factors like temperature, humidity, microbial activity, and exposure to environmental elements.

Fortunately, advancements in DNA techniques have significantly improved the ability to extract and analyze degraded DNA samples. These methods can amplify and sequence even small amounts of degraded DNA, potentially enabling the identification of genetic profiles even after several decades. The genetic code found in the human body can be collected from the skin, blood, saliva, and bone to create a profile. Initially, a significant amount of blood or semen was needed to create DNA profiles. Now it can be picked up from just a few cells that were left behind.

In Windsor, Ontario, a woman was beaten to death in her apartment in 1985. The victim was Judy Sawchuk, who had died of blunt-force trauma. Police had no leads, and the case went cold. One year later, in 1986, a man named Hillman died of a drug overdose. The police had no connection between Hillman and Sawchuk at the time. Then, in 2003, a surprise breakthrough came: a man emerged to whom the late Hillman had apparently confessed to the murder of Judy Sawchuk. In 2006, the police decided to unearth Judy's remains, and through the exhumation, they were able to conclude with DNA evidence that Hillman was, in fact, the murderer of Judy Sawchuk. Cases like this gave the cemetery group hope. However, there was also the possibility that the evidence could clear Egley or point to an unknown suspect.

Once the workers figured they'd dug deep enough, they reversed the backhoe from the grave and used rebar rods to feel out the vault. The steel rods soon connected with the concrete, and they realized they had hit the top of the vault. Two men jumped into the hole, shovels in hand, and went to work, gradually and carefully removing dirt from the vault lid.

Once it was dirt-free, a problem became immediately apparent. A large crack snaked its way across the surface of the concrete cover of the vault.

Everyone watched silently, not daring to vocalize their concerns, clinging to the possibility of hope. With the last pieces of dirt swept off the vault and from around it, the crew secured chains to the concrete structure in preparation to lift it out of the grave. A large tree, the one LuDeen had planted at the grave of her late husband, Parley, prevented them from directly lifting the vault upward, but they tried anyway. They'd come this far.

After ensuring the chains were securely attached, a crane hoisted the vault from the ground. The concrete box swung precariously from side to side, murky water gushing out in torrents from more cracks that were presenting themselves, thus creating a tense and dramatic scene. Over four decades, water had seeped into the ground, dripping not only into the grave but inside the vault holding Loretta's coffin and body. Heidi stood back and watched with wide eyes as the container holding her mother's remains was raised above the burial ground and lowered onto a flatbed truck.

A foot of black sludgy water remained in the hole where the tomb had rested. As viewers peered in, they couldn't help but wonder if the volume of water in the ground would be matched in the vault. The crew placed boards over the open hole and covered it with a tarp to protect it from the elements. It would remain that way until the medical examiner completed his work on Loretta's remains.

As the rest of the group returned to their vehicles, an eerie silence settled over the graveyard, and Heidi hovered in a tender spot between the past and the future, the known and what was to be discovered.

The flatbed truck holding her mother's casket, carrying unanswered questions, shifted into drive and slowly led the procession out of the cemetery. The formation of SUVs, police cars, and news vans weaved through the back country roads and then merged onto the highway for fourteen miles.

Heidi followed the city truck and its precious cargo until it turned toward the search-and-rescue warehouse at the top of Four-Mile Hill. From there, she and Kevin continued past. A void filled her chest, and she felt empty and alone. Removing her mother from her final resting place was justified to convict her killer, but it didn't make it any less difficult. And the possibility remained that it wouldn't be enough to put the killer behind bars.

Long-dormant feelings reared their ugly head. For forty-six years, she had known where her mother was; now it felt like she was being misplaced. She couldn't help but cry out loud, "Mommy, Mommy." She wasn't allowed to be present at the examination but wanted to oversee the transfer of her mother's tomb from the gravesite to the building where the medical examiner would meet the body and do the testing necessary to find any evidence of DNA.

Tomorrow held the promise of revelation. Would it unfold as an open door to clarity or lead down a detour toward an unsolvable mystery? Either way, it would be a long, sleepless night.

•

CHAPTER 27

FINGERS CROSSED

T he medical examiner, Chad Grundy, struggled to process the sight in front of him. The first visual of what was inside the vault could only be described as "guck." Black sludge, water reeking of soil and time, sloshed inside the concrete box holding Loretta Jones's coffin—or what was left of it. But at this point, they couldn't see any sign of the coffin, only black, watery slime.

Sgt. Brewer shook his head. This was far from what they were hoping for. The darkness of the water was eerie and foreboding, but they'd agreed to do this, and they weren't going to back down now.

Chad Grundy hadn't always known this would be his career. His father-in-law's background partly influenced his decision to pursue a career in biology in law enforcement. His father-in-law had held various positions within the state's law enforcement agencies. As part of his job, Grundy's father-in-law worked closely with a local crime lab, and he suggested Grundy might be interested in the line of work. As Grundy began to visit the crime lab, he learned about the Combined DNA Index System (CODIS) and realized he'd found a new passion.

The position required a bachelor's degree in biology, chemistry, or forensic science. When Grundy graduated from the University of Nevada, Las Vegas with a degree in biology, he was hired by the Department of Public Safety directly out of college. He started as a forensic specialist working with the CODIS database and gaining experience studying DNA analysis, serology—the study of body fluids—and crime scene investigation. Eventually, he moved through the Bureau of Forensic Services, becoming a forensic scientist manager in the biology section, working between DNA and fingerprinting.

At the time of the exhumation in 2016, he'd worked as a forensic scientist for fourteen years. Loretta Jones's case marked Grundy's first-ever involvement in an exhumation process. However, he wasn't initially assigned to this case.

A month before the exhumation, Sgt. Brewer had contacted the medical examiner's office to organize the plans for the autopsy, explaining they could take Loretta's remains to Salt Lake City if they needed to. The original ME agreed to the forensic exam, and everything seemed to be unfolding according to plan.

Until the night before the exhumation.

The initial medical examiner phoned Sgt. Brewer and unexpectedly announced that he and his team had decided to back out of the autopsy. The ME's office had held a meeting, and they decided not to participate. Sgt. Brewer pleaded. He had everything prepared, ready to go, but they wouldn't budge. Brewer never learned the reason for the sudden change.

Fortunately, Sgt. Brewer wasn't the type to take no for an answer, and his ability to quickly shift gears came into play.

He had heard of another medical examiner from the area

named Chad Grundy. Small towns had a way like that. He called him on a whim, his first time ever speaking to the man, and crossed his fingers. The exhumation was happening in twelve hours. Was there any possible way Grundy could perform the autopsy? Do DNA testing?

Grundy had encountered Sgt. Brewer in previous inter-actions and was familiar with his name. Brewer had reached out to Grundy, seeking assistance for the crime scene response team, specifically in relation to biology-related matters. While he wasn't versed in exhumation procedures, Chad recognized the potential for DNA recovery from long-standing evidence.

His answer? Yes, he would participate in the exhumation—his first.

After getting approval to perform the autopsy, Grundy joined Sgt. Brewer for the big reveal. As the two men stood in the sheriff's office auxiliary warehouse beside the large concrete vault, wearing only gloves for protection, what hope remained dissipated like air in a balloon. This type of procedure was usu-ally performed in a lab, but since the ME declined to have the body brought to SLC, the cold storage room would have to do, and it worked out to their benefit.

All the water had not drained from the vault, and they real-ized their only solution to reach the coffin was to drill a hole into the side of the concrete vault to drain the liquid. The unspoken question on both their minds was whether there would even be anything left of a wooden coffin.

They rented a Hilti drill, a popular brand known for its du-rability and commonly used in the construction industry. They situated the vault over a drain in the warehouse and a deputy used a long drill bit to bore a hole in the bottom corner of the vault. Once the drill bit reached the other side of the concrete, dark, heavy water gushed out, spewing over the warehouse floor and snaking its way toward the drain. They were both surprised and relieved that there was no foul smell.

As the water began to recede, the level slowly dropped inch by inch. Chad Grundy and Sgt. Brewer started to wonder: Was Loretta's body even still in there? The water was obsidian black, and although it was draining, they still weren't seeing anything.

And then—something poked through the dismal surface. At some point over the last forty-six years, the coffin holding Loretta Jones had collapsed inside the vault; the pressure and weight of water damage was too much for the structure to bear. The coffin had deteriorated so much that only a few pieces of identifiable wood remained, and they floated to the top.

Finally, cloth appeared, wrapped around the splinters and poking through the slush. Decorative blue satin, stained and soaked. It had once cloaked the inside lid of the ornate box, and now it soggily draped over the remains of Loretta Jones.

They didn't see much at first, and it took some time for Brewer and Chad Grundy to remove the desecrated wood and cloth to get to her. After extracting fractured pieces of the coffin, they stood back and observed what remained of the young mother's skeleton.

The initial sight that caught their attention was Loretta's skull. Dark black from time and muck. An unmistakable set of a pinkish-white pair of dentures—both top and bottom—was nestled among the barren bone and stood out in stark contrast. Mud encrusted the cranium orifices, filling the cavities.

It took five men to carefully lift and turn over what was left of the body so they could slide a white sheet beneath her remains.

Gently, each of the men gripped an edge of the sheet and lifted Loretta Jones out of the coffin, laying her on an elongated plastic bin situated beside the vault on the floor.

Although they had hoped for more, the only skeletal parts left of Loretta were her skull and one femur bone. To everyone's dismay, Loretta's skeleton lacked fingernails and had little soft tissue to analyze. Although most of her body had long since decomposed, they discovered some flesh still remaining in her pelvic area.

Grundy didn't think it looked promising. It seemed highly doubtful that any DNA would be left on remains buried in this environment.

Taking a closer look at the fragile skull, Sgt. Brewer, stunned, immediately noticed something he hadn't read in the autopsy report. Dead center in Loretta's forehead was a round hole the exact size of a bullet. Grundy came in for a closer look, and together, they tried to put meaning to this new wound. Had Loretta been shot? How could the original autopsy have missed that detail?

This could alter the course of the entire investigation.

Brewer snapped a photo and sent it to a friend from an archeological department who specialized in Indian artifact sites, including human remains, specifically those that had been under the earth for some time. After reviewing the photo, she identified the hole in Loretta's skull as the result of what has been termed "Chinese water torture." Wikipedia defines this as a "dripping machine." A mentally painful process in which water is slowly dripped onto the scalp, forehead, or face for a prolonged period of time. The process causes fear and mental deterioration on the subject and was first described in the fifteenth century.

Essentially, the prolonged presence of water, a repetitive stream from the lawn's sprinkler system, degraded the exterior of Loretta's skull over an extended period of time, creating a beveled hole through the bone. A constant drip, drip, drip. The specialist suspected the hole had started sometime in the first ten years after Loretta's burial. This was a relief to Brewer and Grundy.

Sgt. Brewer checked for any finger bones that might bear the 1964 Carbon High School class ring that Loretta had been buried with. She'd been wearing it and a green jade ring when she'd been murdered. Heidi was told that when a single woman had a child out of wedlock, an older woman would give her a ring to wear on her wedding finger to avoid unwanted solicitors and rumors. She believed the jade ring was most likely given to Loretta by her maternal grandmother, Delora Daniels, for that reason.

Brewer had seen the jewelry on Loretta's hand in the crime scene photos. What were the odds that she scratched her assailant and some of his skin or DNA remained underneath the rings? Her family believed Loretta had been buried with the two rings, and Sgt. Brewer deduced they must be in the coffin. After they moved Loretta's body into the plastic case, Brewer and Grundy joined forces to dig through the bottom of the vault, searching up to their elbows among the remains of the coffin and the muddy goo. Grundy located Loretta's green ring first and, moments later, her class ring. He believed there was a slim chance of any DNA evidence.

During the exhumation, Grundy's responsibilities included meticulous documentation. He focused on capturing photographs and notes to ensure an accurate record of the evidence present. Grundy aimed to identify potential sources of DNA, knowing that certain types of biological material, like hair and fingernails, could endure after death under certain conditions. He didn't know all the details going in but had hoped to find the assailant's DNA from swabs on Loretta's remains or under her fingernails. However, they found neither hair nor fingernails in the coffin.

Grundy and Brewer had managed to retrieve only a few bones due to the effects of water, decay, and brittleness. Grundy knew that embalming fluid introduced through an artery could complicate efforts to prevent fluid from reaching certain areas. While he lacked knowledge about embalming practices in 1970, he understood that preserving seminal fluid in the vagina might be challenging over time. If samples had been collected at the time of death and stored properly, they could have been successfully tested, as evidenced by tests conducted several decades ago.

Utah State Lab didn't conduct DNA testing until the early nineties. Therefore, any samples would have been sent to the FBI lab for analysis when Loretta first died. Which they were, but unfortunately, the FBI hadn't retained the samples requested for testing.

Things didn't look good. But Sgt. Brewer had invested too much time and emotional energy into this case to simply throw in the towel and walk away.

A local mortuary, Mitchell's Funeral Home, owned by respected businessman Bobby Etzel, planned to donate a new casket for Loretta to be reburied in, but the coffin was in Salt Lake City, and a deputy would need to make the long day trip to retrieve it. Loretta wouldn't be moved into her new resting place until the next day. After Sgt. Brewer finished inspecting

Loretta's remains, he checked his watch. Time had passed. Not just hours from the exhumation but over half a decade since he'd stood on the edge of this case, uncertain about taking a step forward. He was tired.

Brewer pulled his truck inside the warehouse and insisted on staying the night with the remains. His wife joined him, and they slept in the front seat of his truck. As she departed at five thirty the next morning, he was left unaccompanied to continue his vigil.

It was a little unsettling being alone with a corpse, but he tried to sleep. Small beams of light began to illuminate his surroundings. He sat up, looked in the truck's mirror, and caught a shadow as it swept past. Its fleeting presence caused a dramatic shiver down his spine, and he watched as the specter dissipated into nothingness. A reflection of a ghost? His mind playing tricks? He hadn't felt fear. If anything, a strange calm came over him, and he fell back asleep.

Deep down, Brewer knew that the moment the lid of the vault had been lifted, the chances of them finding DNA on Loretta were slim to none. But it didn't matter. Loretta was gone, and although Sgt. Brewer would never have the pleasure of knowing her, he vowed to honor her memory and legacy and close this case once and for all.

With resolve, Sgt. Brewer played his next card. He united with the press to announce the exhumation, emphasizing its purpose: to uncover DNA evidence. However, he chose to keep the fact that no DNA had been found to himself and Heidi.

Despite Tom Egley residing over five hundred miles away, Brewer remained certain that Egley would catch wind of the exhumation. Brewer knew Egley was guilty, and he understood that only a guilty man would hear such news and fear that his days of freedom were numbered.

They might not have Tom Egley's DNA, but Tom didn't know that.

The following morning, Loretta's body was laid to rest in the new casket generously donated by Mitchell's Funeral Home. On this serene day, more family members than law enforcement gathered to return Loretta back to the place she had spent more time deceased than alive. The coffin was adorned with beautiful blue roses, Loretta's favorite color. Heidi delivered a poignant speech and recited her mother's 1963 poem, while Lila's husband, Rick, offered a blessing over the grave.

The day was filled with intense emotions, as if the tragic event had just occurred. Sheriff Jeff Wood, who stood next to Sgt. Brewer, noticed the Salt Lake medium, Lana, standing back from the crowd. He watched as a beautiful monarch butterfly landed softly on her hand. She could not attend the exhumation, so she made it a point to be at the reinterment, which meant a lot to Heidi. Walking up to Heidi, who stood near the grave, Lana held out her hand, showing Heidi the heart rock, which was the twin to the one she had given Heidi years ago. "I'd like this to go with your mother," Lana said. So Bobby Etzel, the funeral director, opened the casket lid enough to place the rock inside with Loretta. The two girls held hands, and nothing more needed to be said.

Gravestones of diverse shapes and sizes stood in solemn rows, all oriented eastward. Each one whispered a distinct tale of lives that had once graced the earth. A gentle breeze carried the soft rustle of leaves, creating a calming melody. Flower-adorned plots added vibrant splashes of color to the grassy landscape. The air, imbued with a quiet reflection, invited visitors to remember those who rested peacefully beneath the sheltering branches.

The press was among those who had returned the day after the exhumation to gather for the reinterment. They slowly departed after collecting last-minute details for the nightly news. Heidi and Kevin lingered until they were the sole figures in the quiet cemetery. Hand in hand, they found solace in the belief that Loretta again lay at peace beneath the shade of the grand tree, reunited with her parents.

CHAPTER 28

EMDR

W ith the knowledge that the exhumation had not produced any DNA as hoped, Heidi continued to seek out
avenues that might aid her in remembering something
that would be helpful to the case. Brewer's coworker, Detective
Wally Hendricks, suggested Eye Movement Desensitization and
Reprocessing (EMDR) therapy. This is a mental health treatment technique that involves moving your eyes a specific way
while you process traumatic memories. EMDR's goal is to help
a person heal from trauma or other distressing life experiences.
Research has shown that EMDR therapy is incredibly effective
for those who have lived through trauma or suffer from PTSD.
Many experienced immediate benefits, and most reported no
relapses in symptoms months after treatment had ended.

It was the Fourth of July weekend, 2016, and most people
were getting ready for camping or picnics to help escape the
heat of summer. Heidi had found an EMDR therapist in Price,
and she and Kevin walked into the office of Kim Bradley*, a

little nervous but a lot hopeful. The detectives hoped that some hidden memory would come forth, giving them a new lead.

For the next two and a half hours, Kevin waited restlessly in the lobby. He could hear Heidi speaking loudly in a childlike voice from behind the closed door where Heidi met with Kim. A sound like a small animal whimpering in distress put him on the edge of his seat. Should he interrupt or sit tight? He could only imagine how tough this must be on his new wife, but he knew she wanted to do this, so he sat uneasily and tried to relax.

In the next room, Kim moved her finger back and forth as Heidi followed it with her eyes. This would continue for a few minutes, and then Heidi was asked what she could remember. At first, nothing came to Heidi's mind, and the finger gesture was repeated.

"What do you remember?"

"Nothing."

Then, after the third time, she remembered thinking, *Holy cow, where is this coming from?*

A memory of Tom surfaced, and she could smell cigarettes and alcohol.

The session went on, and Kevin continued to sit and pace as he listened painfully to the sound of Heidi's muffled screams and cries echoing through the wall. Checking his watch every five minutes until the hour was up did nothing to help the time pass faster.

After, Heidi did not listen to the recorded session, but Sgt. Brewer and Det. Hendricks did. They both agreed it was bringing up memories associated with Tom. Still, because Tom had been to her home several times, Brewer felt the memories were not specific to the night of the murder.

In criminal law, the use of repressed memories as evidence is generally met with skepticism and may not be admitted if the court finds them unreliable or if the process of recovering the memories involves suggestive techniques.

The detectives were hoping that Heidi might have a solid memory of what made her look through the keyhole and if she had any recall that a murder was happening on the other side of her door. Heidi knew Tom well enough to know his name, and they believed she knew him enough to identify him when she was four years old. Had she heard his voice and felt at ease enough to fall asleep knowing her mother was with someone she knew?

Because this technique puts the client in a fugue-like state, Kim asked Heidi to contact her if memories surfaced that she needed help processing. It could happen that her subconscious would continue to bring up traumatic memories for some time. Heidi texted her, letting her know she was okay, and Kim was glad to hear from her.

Although nothing surfaced to aid the case, Heidi found the experience profoundly therapeutic. It served as a necessary release and allowed her to unburden herself from the weight of fear and grief that had been holding her back, preventing her from moving forward.

After the session, when Heidi walked out of the door and saw the look on Kevin's worried face, she knew that something had happened. The black mascara running down her face told him what he knew, but she didn't. She had been crying and had not realized it until that moment.

CHAPTER 29

DYING DECLARATION

It sounded like something straight out of a Hollywood movie. A cryptic clue in a box office thriller. That was the only way Sgt. Brewer could describe the possibility that Loretta had left a message in her dying moments.

Not long after the exhumation, Heidi received a Facebook message from one of her sister's old friends. The message was ambiguous: "I have something to tell Brewer. Do you think it would be okay to contact him?" So, a few days later, Sgt. Brewer received a phone call from a woman named Linda, and what she had to say would ignite the stalled case back into motion.

Brewer, coping with the disappointment of the absence of DNA evidence, remained receptive to any potential new leads. Despite his frustration and the presence of a good luck charm hanging in his car, his detective instincts demanded logic and irrefutable proof to secure an arrest. Nevertheless, feeling the weight of the case, he was not averse to entertaining even far-fetched information that could inject a glimmer of hope. Thus, he agreed to meet with Linda Lloyd.

Linda was the friend of Loretta's sister Carolyn, who, in 1970, after starting college, moved out of her parents' house and moved in with LuDeen and Parley, where she'd continued to live while pursuing higher education.

After Loretta's murder, Linda accompanied her surrogate family back to the house to assist in gathering the belongings of then four-year-old Heidi. Parley instructed the girls not to go into the living room where Loretta had been murdered, but Linda's morbid curiosity got the best of her.

"And that's where I saw it," she told Sgt. Brewer.

"Saw what exactly?" Sgt. Brewer asked.

"The letters *T* and *O* written in blood on the living room floor."

Brewer hoped the look on his face wasn't showing her how crazy he thought this revelation sounded.

"Did you not know that Loretta wrote the killer's name in blood?" Linda asked the speechless detective, whose deer-in-the-headlights expression gave her the answer.

Could it be possible that nearly a decade's worth of investigation would lead to an ending like this? As she was dying, had Loretta been mindful enough to leave behind the name of her killer? *T* and *O* for Tom Egley. It seemed so straightforward, and if it was true, Sgt. Brewer wasn't sure how he could have missed it, how all of the investigators had missed it. Of course, Brewer needed to validate her story before he could act on his elation.

They met at Linda's home in Price, and he had her draw from memory the image of the letters she remembered from the crime scene, including the general area where they'd been scrawled on the floor. Linda was happy to oblige, even drawing what the original linoleum looked like. Armed with this piece of witness evidence, Brewer took the drawing back to the sheriff's office and sifted through the binder of research, documents, files, and photographs that Heidi had provided him pertaining to the case. Linda had assumed Brewer already had this evidence from old case files, so she had not come forward earlier.

There was one black-and-white photograph that stood out in particular. In it, a four- or five-year-old Heidi stood in the living room where her mother had been murdered. She was wearing a winter coat, her face emotionless as she stood behind the chalked outline and a remnant of a stain on the floor. The spot where her mother had taken her last breath. That photo had always bothered Brewer. Why would someone take that little girl, the daughter of the murder victim, and take a picture of her standing next to her mother's traced frame?

As an adult, Heidi didn't remember returning to the house, but she assumed it had happened later in the year because she was wearing warmer clothing. She believed this photograph was taken when she accompanied her grandparents to the house to get the remainder of her things so the house could finally be cleaned and rented out. Her grandfather, who snapped the photo, did not mean to capture Heidi in it. As the camera clicked, she had just entered the room. The photo was not taken carelessly but more accidentally. And those who knew Parley would never question his intentions.

Brewer looked closely, tilting the photo through different angles and enlarging it on his computer. It took him some time, but sure enough, right there in the crime scene photograph, near where Heidi stood, was the faint print of the letters T and O—just like Linda had drawn it. Unbelievable! It sounded too easy, too much like a preposterous *Perry Mason* episode.

How had so many people missed this? How much more evidence was out there that had been overlooked? And now what?

Brewer reflected back to some details from the preliminary hearing. The description of the blood on the floor being smeared as if Loretta had moved her hand back and forth, and also that Officer Barry Bryner had been one of the young deputies first to the scene. So many original investigators from the case had either moved or were deceased, so Brewer knew his chances of locating Bryner were slim. But the luck of the leprechaun was on his side, and he was able to locate the former Carbon County sheriff Bryner, who later passed away in 2018.

Sgt. Brewer wanted to know if Bryner recalled any of these details from the scene, so he phoned him and casually asked if he knew anything about Loretta writing her killer's name in blood. Brewer didn't want to give any information to Bryner that he might not know, but to his surprise, without hesitation, Bryner confirmed everything, explaining in detail what he'd seen with his own eyes. Loretta Jones was still lying in a pool of blood when Bryner arrived at the scene. And there, on the floor beside her, were the letters *T* and *O* smeared within a more significant bloodstain. Nothing about this detail had been documented, and if it had, it would be in the missing files.

And why, if both Officer Barry Bryner and Linda Lloyd had witnessed the letters *TO* scrawled in blood next to Loretta's body, had this not been used as a clue in the 1970 investigation? Brewer's theory was that law enforcement did see the cryptic alphabet message but were at a loss at how to use it in their case. He also stated that Linda Lloyd first learned about the bloody *TO* at school. That detail had leaked out of the police department and into the general public, and it was on everyone's tongues. So when she went to the house with the family to gather items for Heidi, she made it a point to verify the rumor. It was a fact but a clue that attorneys at the time felt might hurt them in court as the defense could argue that *TO* could refer to many names, Tony, Todd, Toby, etc.

A well-known Italian murder case was reopened after discovering a message apparently written in blood by a dying victim, leading to the arrest of a suspect fourteen years later. Vincenzo Morici, a surgeon, was accused of stabbing his wife to death in 1993. Recent technology revealed that what was initially thought to be a bloodstain could have been a desperate attempt to identify the killer. Antonella Falcidia, also a doctor, was found dead in their flat with twenty-three stab wounds. The investigation, aided by digitally enhanced images, revealed markings resembling letters in the middle of Dr. Morici's name, *ENZ*.

As Brewer continued scrutinizing the vintage photograph, thoughts of Loretta's dying act moved him. Her final actions spoke volumes about Loretta's character as a person and a mother. Sgt. Brewer marveled at her strength in subduing her fear enough to prioritize leaving behind a clue that could potentially aid in solving her own murder and bring closure to others. A strength that refused to fade even in her final moments of unimaginable terror.

Loretta wasn't just brave; she was fiercely protective of Heidi. Even though it must have been painful, she never once cried out, doubtless saving her daughter from a similar fate.

While Sgt. Brewer was trying to figure out how this odd-shaped piece of the puzzle fit and how he could use it to bolster the case, the DNA news hit the target!

CHAPTER 30

NEWS TRAVELS FAST

He knows." Bullseye!

Though the initial strategy was to spread the news about the potential DNA discovery through newspapers, the whisper of murder seemed to propel the information much faster through the intricate channels of the grapevine.

Sgt. Brewer quickly got wind of Tom Egley's increasing nervousness surrounding the case. Not long after Brewer announced the exhumation to the press and by proxy to Egley, Heidi heard from an old friend, Teresa Dalton*, who lived in Rocky Ford, Colorado.

Teresa received a call from a woman Tom had assisted on their farm, offering rides into town for her and her husband. In their conversation, Teresa learned that Tom was concerned about detectives from Utah coming to arrest him. He had requested the woman watch over his dogs in case of his absence. When Teresa heard this, she called Heidi. Heidi informed Detective Brewer, who contacted the woman, who relayed the same information.

"Is he suicidal?" he asked her. She didn't get that impression from Egley, but Brewer decided to take action and contacted the Rocky Ford Police Department and explained who he was and the current situation. If the police department received any disturbance from Tom Egley's address, they needed to use caution, as Egley's behavior was unpredictable and possibly dangerous. Authorities were searching for DNA, after all. Was Tom now planning a trip to avoid being caught up in the chaos, a guilty man, weighed down by his past, refusing to take accountability for his crime? Or perhaps his motive was more final than that. Perhaps he planned to take his own life to avoid facing repercussions.

The exhumation and reinterment story would unfold across various mediums: local news segments, newspaper headlines, radio broadcasts, and a featured article in the Rocky Ford *Daily Gazette*. The widespread coverage undoubtedly intensified the scrutiny on Tom, amplifying the pressure he must have been feeling about the potential discovery of his DNA on the victim's body.

KOAL Radio Broadcast—June 8, 2016

Loretta Jones was once again laid to rest Wednesday in the Elmo town cemetery after her body was exhumed Tuesday afternoon for evidence in a cold case related to her death in 1970.

"We exhumed the body of Loretta Jones, a cold case from 1970 that I have been investigating for seven years, and we took the next steps in the investigation," said Carbon County Sergeant David Brewer. "Hopefully, with modern technology the way it is versus 1970, we can get a DNA profile for a suspect in this case."

ETV News, Author, Shannon Childs—June 9, 2016
UPDATE Body Exhumed in Elmo with the Hope of Solving Cold
Case Murder

ETV/Progress, Author, Richard Shaw—June 14, 2016
*LORETTA JONES' BODY IN ELMO REBURIED AFTER BEING
EXHUMED FOR EVIDENCE*
*The body of Loretta Jones was re-interred in the Elmo town cemetery
on Wednesday afternoon, after being exhumed earlier for evidence
concerning her death almost 46 years ago. Jones was murdered in
July of 1970 and while the case against a suspect was dismissed at the
time, the idea that someday justice might be served grew closer this
week, after almost seven years of investigation by the Carbon County
Sheriff's Office.*

Brewer knew he was on the right path. But he'd struggled with this case for so long that now, like a weary sailor battling a relentless storm, his spirit was dimmed by crashing waves of doubt. The end goal, solving Loretta Jones's case, often seemed eternally distant, a mocking reminder of an endless journey. And now a gust of determination had filled his sails. The mist of uncertainty had dissipated, unveiling the distant shore—the finish line—now vivid and within reach. Sgt. Brewer found himself on the final stretch, with the wind at his back and the sensation of success waiting in the air.

Although a phone call from the Rocky Ford Police Department never came in, a different call did.

On the day of the reinterment, Brewer was sitting in his vehicle when his phone rang. "Is this Detective Brewer?" the woman's voice asked over the speaker. The woman identified herself as Karen Cox*, a neighbor of Tom Egley. She recounted a disturbing incident to Brewer, describing how she found Tom attempting to cut her tree down because some of its branches were hanging over into his yard. She confronted him, and with a mixture of fear and disbelief, she recalled how his demeanor shifted suddenly, his face purple with rage as he advanced toward her swinging the chain saw.

"I just want you to know you've got the right guy," she told Brewer.

Tom Egley was the custodian of his mother's estate but had never put the property in his name. When his daughter Mary showed up at his house one time, she asked about her grandmother, Tom's mother, and Tom said her grandmother was dead, which turned out to be a lie. Still, when his mother eventually did pass, Tom inherited the run-down trailer and became her estate's conservator.

At best, his relationship with his mother was strained and broken. Mary Egley Williams had practically raised Tom's son, Tom Jr., when Tom would drop him off and disappear for periods of time. Tom had many ex-wives, abandoned children, and few stable relationships.

Many described Tom as a recluse. He had few friends and avoided most contact with his family. However, he was friends with a man whose daughter, Karen Cox, lived down the street from him.

Tom Egley had been predominantly alone for the better part of the last two decades. His single-wide mobile home was completely paid off, so other than utilities, seventy-six-year-old Tom had few bills and lived entirely off Social Security. In his spare time, he worked as a farmhand on a nearby property and, interestingly enough, read true crime as a hobby. (Earlier in his life, in the aftermath of Loretta's murder, investigators noted that he had piles of true crime and *True Detective* magazines in his residence.) He smoked heavily and eventually became diagnosed with cancer and cataracts.

Egley had a drinking buddy down the road, and the two of them would often indulge together. Rumor had it that at one point, Tom drunkenly confessed to this friend that he had killed a person in the past, but like most rumors, it was unsubstantiated and never verified.

But what if Karen could verify it? She mulled over the connection between his temper and the possibility of DNA. She felt Tom trusted her, and perhaps he would confide in her. The thought of Loretta's cold case lingered in her mind, igniting a readiness to assist in any way possible.

CHAPTER 31

THE CONFESSION

B rewer had one last meeting with the AG's office after the exhumation in an effort to rally support after Mr. Strate decided not to prosecute. During this roundtable discussion, one of the attorneys made an obvious suggestion: the case could easily be closed if Brewer could get a confession.

Brewer had already interviewed Egley in 2010 and was unsuccessful in eliciting an admission. So it wasn't like he hadn't tried. He'd spent all this time dredging up the past for evidence and statements, exploring the crime's external circumstances, but he needed the words from one of the only two people who knew what happened that night: Tom Egley.

How could Brewer somehow get him to admit to the crime?

Over time, Karen's interaction with Egley increased. She kept Brewer informed of their conversations, which up to this point were mostly about local events, the weather, etc. She let Brewer in on her idea to get Egley talking about Loretta's murder. When Sgt. Brewer heard Karen's plan, he admittedly hesitated. This was everything he'd been waiting for—an actual possibility of getting a confession from the murderer. An opportunity like this wouldn't knock twice, so why not give it a try? Karen was more than willing to help, and Egley trusted her for whatever reason. So, over the course of several weeks, Karen gradually began visiting Egley's house and recording their conversations on her cell phone.

To get a confession out of him, she would have to handle him without him picking up on what she was doing. By recording all their interactions, Karen not only guaranteed the likelihood of capturing Tom's confession, but it would ensure transparency in the process, ideally revealing to prosecutors and future jury members that Karen didn't cross a line into manipulating or entrapping Tom into confessing.

By tapping into empathy, Karen gained an advantage formal interrogations often lack. Rather than coercing Tom's confession, she became a friend, a confidante, and someone he could trust.

Tom liked to feel important and heard. Perhaps a sympathetic ear and someone to validate him as a human being would appeal to his empathic side. Karen knew exactly how to do that without Tom suspecting she was working with the police, and he continued to open his door to their visits.

For her safety, Karen would call Sgt. Brewer when she arrived at Tom's house and immediately called him again when she left. If she didn't call him back within a certain amount of time, say within an hour, Sgt. Brewer assured he would send in the cavalry.

After a few weeks of this, Karen gradually started hinting to Tom that the police had found crucial information about the killer from the exhumation.

She initiated a plan and told Tom this story:

During a training that her husband, who was a police officer, was attending in Utah, Tom Egley had become the topic of the class as a possible suspect in the murder of Loretta Jones. She told her husband that because she'd known Tom for twenty-plus years, she wanted to know what was going on with the case. Karen's husband told her that Tom was in a bad spot. What exactly did the cops have on him? Then her husband dropped a bombshell. According to him, the police department still had the swabs from Loretta's autopsy, giving them DNA from the night of the killing.

Of course, none of Karen's stories were true except for the fact that her husband was a police officer.

However, at this point, she'd built a rapport with Tom so that he didn't question what she said. But he did question something else.

Tom flatly responded to Karen, "Well, I don't know how they can have DNA."

For Karen, his words were a pivotal moment. "It totally blew me away." It was the first time Tom had voluntarily talked about an aspect of the crime.

Two days later, Karen returned to Tom's house, and to her surprise—and delight—Tom started talking.

Egley explained how, on the night of Loretta's murder, he'd been in the neighborhood and knocked on Loretta's door. Loretta answered, greeted him, and let him inside.

The following is an exact transcript of the conversation Karen recorded on her mobile phone.

> Karen: Okay. And the door closed, and then what? What would you think happened? If you had to guess, what do you think happened?

Tom: I was turned down for sex.

Karen: Okay. And that made you feel how?

Tom: Like shit. And when she came back, I stabbed her.

It had happened, the moment Karen had been waiting for. And yet the impact of Tom's words hadn't fully hit her. All she could think about was the tone of Tom's voice. "His voice never changed, and I think that is what got me," Karen recalled. "He admitted to stabbing Loretta Jones as if he were talking about Sunday dinner." He then added that Loretta hadn't died immediately, and she lay on the floor moaning.

Karen: Did you have sex with her?

Tom: Of course I had sex with her.

To Karen's shock, Tom added something extra to that confession.

Tom: It was consensual.

Karen: Tom, you stabbed her. How was that consensual?

Tom: She didn't tell me no.

That statement took Karen a while to process. "I couldn't believe what I'd just heard," she stated.

Karen: So you remember having sex with her, and then what?

Tom: I lost it. I cut her throat, and I left.

And there it was. Forty-six years after Loretta Jones's murder, the man who killed her had finally admitted it. And his neighbor, Karen Cox, had proof.

While Karen wasn't completely sure why Tom didn't harm Heidi, she believed that had Loretta screamed, Heidi would have come out of the bedroom and witnessed Tom in the act. She believed wholeheartedly that Tom would have killed Heidi if that had happened.

And that night, Loretta's silence had saved her daughter's life. Tom reported that at one point, when he and Loretta were arguing, Loretta told him they needed to be quiet so they didn't wake up Heidi, and Loretta closed the back bedroom door so her daughter wouldn't hear them fighting.

Tom had decided he was going to get what he wanted from Loretta. He couldn't stand being denied sex. He waited for her to turn her back on him, and that was when he grabbed his knife. He waited for her to come from the kitchen, and then he stabbed her repeatedly before raping her and eventually killing her.

Tom explained that he kept the knife and some other pieces of evidence in the basement of the building he lived in, and then later when he moved out of the hotel, he tossed the murder weapon into the river behind the hotel in Helper.

Tom described everything with zero remorse, said Karen. "I don't believe he even cared."

Karen, testing her luck, suggested Tom confess to the police. He was living in Rocky Ford and didn't want to cross state lines into Utah, fearing being arrested. Tom believed he was going to get off if he stayed in Colorado. Karen explained to him that it would be fine, that this was an old case, one they didn't care too much about. The police just wanted closure.

Tom agreed to talk to the police but asked for a couple of promises: 1) He wouldn't get arrested and 2) Heidi wouldn't get his single-wide trailer. He feared that Heidi would go after everything he owned in a lawsuit.

Karen suggested calling up Sgt. Brewer and talking to him on the phone so they could plan to meet up. Little did Tom know, Sgt. Brewer and Detective Hendricks had set up headquarters in the conference room of a hotel nearby in La Junta, fifteen miles from Rocky Ford, not in Utah, as she had told him. After Karen talked to Tom, she would go to the hotel, meet them, and brief them on anything she had learned. They listened to the recordings several times for a few days, finding nothing substantial. Tom agreed, and Karen made the call, crossed her fingers, and prayed that Sgt. Brewer would answer.

He did.

She had Sgt. Brewer on speaker, so she spoke quickly before he accidentally revealed they were working together.

Karen explained to Sgt. Brewer that she was sitting with Tom Egley and understood that Brewer wanted to investigate the Loretta Jones case. Essentially, she played dumb, explaining to Brewer that Tom Egley would really like to talk about Loretta Jones. Pretending to have Tom's back, Karen explained that he couldn't leave the house because of his animals.

Only fifteen miles away, Sgt. Brewer picked up on what Karen was getting at. He said that today would be hard as he probably wouldn't be able to get a flight out. He inquired about the next day and asked if there was an airport nearby. Karen suggested the La Junta airport, and Sgt. Brewer agreed, saying he would look and see when he could be there the next day, possibly in the afternoon. He wanted to get a game plan in place before he met with Egley.

Afterward, Karen called the detectives after leaving Tom's, who were eating dinner at a small home-style restaurant. Detective Hendricks took the call and gave Brewer the look that said, "We need to go. Now." So they left their dinner, paid, and returned to the hotel. Karen and her husband arrived at the hotel fifteen minutes later. In somewhat of a shock over what had just occurred, she excitedly told them, "I got it on tape. He admitted to slitting her throat."

Karen proudly handed over the valuable phone recording to Brewer. Was he finally in possession of the final puzzle piece?

CHAPTER 32

"I STOOD UP AND STABBED HER."

rewer recalls that after seven years of ups and downs with this case, he didn't initially feel overly excited. It wasn't until they played the confession again that he got goose bumps. He then saved the confession on every recording device they had so as not to lose the evidence if Karen's phone glitched and deleted it.

The detectives each made calls to their most respected law enforcement colleagues. Brewer called his mentor, Vince Meister, the Utah attorney. Vince listened as his friend excitedly told him the news and encouraged Brewer to move forward. Vince was the kind of guy who had so much wisdom and would have rolled the dice and taken this case to court long ago if he had been the attorney in Carbon County.

"Do we have enough to take him to court?" Brewer asked Vince.

His advice to Brewer was, "Getting a confession in person is your best bet, and do some damage control before Tom talks. It's crucial to address and retract any promises made by Karen.

Tom cannot be assured that he won't be held accountable; he must be made aware that he needs to answer for his actions."

Hendricks called his guy, Wallentine, who was the chief of police in West Jordan. He was elated to hear they had a confession as well.

Twenty-four hours later, the second part of the plan was executed, and Brewer's agenda listed only two action items. 1) Address Tom's requests 2) Obtain a face-to-face confession.

Karen told Tom that Sgt. Brewer was flying in from Carbon County and explained that no one would mess with or touch him and that he would not be arrested. That day, by coincidence, a plane flew over Tom's house while Karen was there, and he looked up and said, "That must be them." Leaving Tom, she went to the hotel and picked up Brewer and Hendricks and drove them to Tom's house. Brewer played along when Egley met them outside, joking about being jet-lagged, implying that they'd just arrived in town. They went inside with Egley, and Karen assured him again that it was okay to tell the truth, that Tom wouldn't face any penalties, and that things were going to be okay.

Sitting down inside the musty trailer, Brewer swiftly navigated the situation and did some damage control before Tom divulged too much information. Brewer had invited Hendricks to accompany him to Colorado due to his exceptional interviewing skills, but since Karen would be asking questions, he created a "recipe" for her to follow. However, she had drifted from the script and made assurances to Tom that they could not keep. Tom was told that whatever he told them could be used against him and that he would likely be arrested. But they could keep their promise that it wouldn't be today. This cleared up Tom's first request.

Brewer had the foresight to contact Heidi and have her fax the legally signed document stating she would not take Tom's home or sue him civically. He wanted to have it in hand when he met with Tom so there would be no delay in a second confession. This met his second request.

Now that Tom's demands were addressed, Brewer wanted to get what he had been waiting for all these years, so he leaned forward and carefully pressed the record button, ensuring Egley didn't speak until the red light blinked. When he finally pushed the Stop button, Brewer had a full confession from Thomas Edward Egley. He had murdered Loretta Jones.

The following is Tom's written statement, which was notarized by the State of Colorado and entered into evidence in State v. Egley, Chapter 12—021.

I went to Loretta's house and knocked on the door. She let me in.

We sat down on the couch and talked. About what I don't recall.

After we had talked for a while we may have had sex on the couch I don't remember.

She got up from the couch and went into what I think was the kitchen. While she was in the kitchen I asked her for sex and she turned me down by saying No.

I then reached into my pocket and took out my knife. When she returned I stood up and stabbed her with it.

She fell in front of the couch where I cut her throat.

I don't remember stabbing her more than once and I surely don't remember cut her panties. After cutting her throat I then left for home.

I didn't know that her daughter was there. Because I never did see her I thought Loretta was home by herself.

I'm sorry that she had to find her mother like that.

More than she'll ever know I'm terribly sorry with all my heart for taking her mother away from her.

When I say I don't remember I just don't. After 46 years I've been as honest as I can be.

Tom Egley 8/11/16

After decades of guarding a secret, his fate was now in the hands of the State of Utah.

CHAPTER 33

THE ARREST

The details of the murder were finally captured on Brewer's cell phone and solidified in a formal statement. Brewer had the evidence he'd been seeking. At last!

Because the Carbon County Sheriff's Office had no arresting powers in Colorado and no jurisdiction, they could not arrest Tom but told him they could not promise he wouldn't have to account for his actions in some way. So they left him to sit alone and contemplate his fate while they headed straight to the liquor store, each detective purchasing their own brand of poison to celebrate the long-sought-after victory. But Brewer needed to make a very important phone call before they left the parking lot.

With steady hands, he dialed the familiar number. "Heidi, Tom has a message for you. He's sorry he killed your mother." Her reaction to this day gives the veteran detective goose bumps. She cried, she screamed, she danced for joy. It was a good call to make!

After returning to the hotel, they poured themselves a drink and began sorting through their notes. Surprisingly, morning arrived without any lingering headaches. Before heading back to Utah, they made a pit stop at a convenience store in Brewer's inconspicuous truck to grab Hendricks a Mtn Dew for the journey.

As Hendricks went inside the store, Brewer caught sight of an aging vehicle pulling up beside him on the passenger side. To his dismay, it was Tom Egley. Brewer quickly slid down in his seat, subtly reversed the truck using just his mirrors, and parked discreetly on the opposite side of the building.

Anxiously, Brewer observed as Tom exited his vehicle, heading straight for the store entrance. Just then, Hendricks emerged from the store, and in the hustle, their shoulders bumped. At six feet tall, Detective Hendricks was hard to miss.

With Tom now inside the store, Brewer honked the horn to alert Hendricks of his new location. A flustered Hendricks jumped into the truck and, thinking Brewer was playing a prank on him, chastised him with a few choice words.

"That was Tom you just bumped into," Brewer told him. They had not recognized each other, and that was a good thing, as Tom had been led to believe the pair left the state by plane yesterday. This encounter could have blown the trust that Karen had cultivated.

There had been another close call when Brewer, having transferred a prescription to Colorado, was recognized by a woman in the store. "You're Sgt. Brewer from Utah." As it turned out, she was someone Heidi knew. Brewer promptly contacted Heidi and instructed her to contact the woman, asking her not to disclose their presence in town to anyone.

Back in Utah, the recorded confession obtained on July 16, 2016, was handed over to the Carbon County attorney. Even then, it took time for the pieces to fall into place, but Egley was finally arrested for the murder of Loretta Jones.

Tom called Karen the morning of the arrest, hoping to talk. She told him she had to run to Walmart, because she knew the marshals were on their way to his house. Tom sat alone for a short time before his dogs alerted him to visitors on the porch. He met them at the door, knowing they were there to arrest him. Without resistance, he extended his hands and accepted the cold embrace of the metal cuffs. Outside, he paused to pat the heads of his loyal dogs as best as his restraints allowed, a silent farewell. Head bowed, he walked toward the waiting van. That day marked the last day of his freedom.

Karen didn't hear from Tom until later that day when he called her from the jailhouse.

Although, on some level, Tom had to know that his confession to Karen was what put him behind bars, he still trusted her. His call instructed her to go to his house, get his keys out of the refrigerator freezer on the back porch, and close up the house. Then he had a lawyer meet Karen at the house and sign over the power of attorney to her. This way, his bills would get paid, and she could take care of things for him, including his dogs, which she eventually found new homes for.

Heidi, meanwhile, couldn't have been happier. "It's like a dream come true. After forty-six years and telling my story over and over again, finally, not only is he caught, but he confessed." And to celebrate her friend's happiness, Heidi's friend Lulu sent her forty-six blue roses. One for every year her mom's case went unsolved.

───────────────

Tom Egley was held on a million-dollar bond in Otero County, Colorado, and appeared before 16th Judicial District Judge Michael Schiferl at his extradition hearing. With the advice of his public defender, Rusty Zane, Egley signed the extradition papers that would return him to Utah, the state he'd left not long after Loretta's murder more than four decades ago. During the extradition hearing, Judge Schiferl set a subsequent hearing for seven to ten days to confirm that Egley had been transferred to Utah, where he would be held in solitary confinement. The Utah AG's office sent the US marshals, who handle extraditions between states, to transport Egley from Colorado to Utah.

According to the court documents filed for his arrest, Egley allegedly entered the home of Loretta Jones, twenty-three, in Price, Utah, on July 30, 1970. Following Egley's recorded confession, the documents listed that Egley had stabbed Jones after she had turned him down for sex. Therefore, once back in Utah, Egley would face charges of criminal homicide, murder in the second degree, and rape in the first degree.

After his extradition back to Utah on August 26, 2016, Egley, who was seventy-six years old at the time, appeared before a 7th District Court video from a Carbon County jail. Represented by David Allred, Egley was officially charged with the rape and murder of Loretta Jones. Although Egley confirmed that he understood the charges, he didn't enter a plea. The purpose of this hearing was to allow Tom to fill out the paperwork about the case so the court could assign him a defense attorney. He stayed incarcerated in the Carbon County jail from September until November.

The novel idea of purchasing pink handcuffs came to Brewer after learning Loretta had been wearing pink pedal pushers when she was murdered. He actually purchased two sets of pink handcuffs. The first ones were put on Egley's wrists by Sgt. Brewer, after the marshals arrested him and handed him off to Brewer at the Salt Lake City airport. They were used again when Egley was escorted to Utah State Prison. The other set hangs on Heidi's living room wall and was made into a plaque given to her by Sgt. Brewer and Dr. Walton with the inscription *Sit pax Have vas*, which translated from Latin to English means "Let peace be your vessel."

Heidi also possessed a photograph of Tom being hand-cuffed by the marshals, a unique gift that Brewer and Hendricks surprised her with during a visit to her home. They had fabricated their reason for the visit, claiming they needed her to sign some papers. The photo shows Tom, head down and clad in an orange jumpsuit and handcuffs, being walked toward Utah State Prison. The photo of her receiving the gift, is of the three of them, smiling and at peace.

Heidi Jones-Asay attended the hearing and sat in the court-room as Tom appeared on the video conference. Although her mother's murderer wasn't in the room with her, hearing him speak was enough to trigger her. "Just hearing the sound of his voice after all this time, it fills you with a bunch of emotion."

Although Heidi was too young to remember the court hearing during Egley's first arrest, she still carried around a 1970 newspaper clipping covering Egley's initial release from custody. Now, all this time later, Heidi was confident that the next newspaper clipping she'd hold would detail Egley's imprisonment.

Heidi was hopeful that this journey finally had an ending. After the hearing, she told the Salt Lake Tribune, "It seems like it's the beginning of the end now. I know it's going to be an emotional roller coaster for the next month or two, but I'm ready for it now."

Sgt. Brewer wasn't as certain. Even with the recorded confessions and Tom's arrest, the excitement of solving the case hadn't fully sunk in for him. As he relayed to the *Tribune*, "I don't want to jinx things by getting too excited yet. But I guess now that the court proceedings have begun, I can feel a little more enthusiastic. Eventually, it'll sink in."

Brewer understood that while he had obtained a confession from Tom, having corroborating evidence to support Tom's story would be advantageous for the court proceedings so while in Helper one day, Brewer thought, why not check into a claim Tom made himself? Egley told detectives on the day of his confession, that he had hidden the bloody clothes he wore the night of the murder in the basement where he had been working. Brewer knew the place to be the old Sportsman Club, which now houses the Clampers (a fraternal organization dedicated to the preservation of the heritage of the American West). He gained their permission to search the old dusty basement and crept around, fighting off cobwebs as he looked in every crook and corner, coming up empty-handed. Brewer recalled that in one of Egley's initial interviews, he told detectives he had thrown the knife (the murder weapon) in the river, and although there was never a current attempt to locate it, Brewer believed it to be the truth. The knife was never found.

Throughout the fall of 2016, hearings surrounding the case continued until October 11. Through plea negotiations, Tom Egley agreed to plead guilty on the condition that the rape charge was dismissed. Egley pled guilty to criminal homicide and murder in the second degree.

The final step awaited: the sentencing of Thomas Edward Egley. This would be Heidi's moment to face the man who took away her mother, robbing her of a lifetime filled with memories and love. She would get a voice for herself and for the mother she had never given up on.

CHAPTER 34

Even Monsters Grow Old

T he old courthouse, constructed in 1958 by Loretta Jones's father during the Cold War, was originally designed as a fallout shelter and was primarily made of cement. The walls were fitted with bars and used as the sheriff's office, with jail cells on two floors. Later on, the building underwent a transformation into a courthouse. Given the constrained space, closets were repurposed as offices, former cells became storage closets, and a significant portion of the basement was transformed into a legal library. But after fifty-seven years of use, in 2015, the old building was demolished to make room for a new, more modern courthouse. The replacement building, constructed directly behind the original, was packed on the morning of November 22, 2016, which was also Kevin's birthday. Heidi Jones-Asay gathered with family, friends, sheriff's deputies, and reporters to hear the case against Thomas Edward Egley.

Recognizing Loretta's absence, Heidi showcased a photo of her deceased mother in an elegant frame and propped it up on an easel, visible to everyone in the courtroom.

Although he had finally admitted in a court of law that he had killed Loretta Jones forty-six years earlier, there still seemed to be a disconnect, like he hadn't fully grasped why any of this really mattered. The Department of Corrections prepared a report detailing the investigation, and at his sentencing hearing, Egley confirmed that it was correct.

When Judge George Harmond asked Egley if he understood the plea deal, Egley confirmed he understood but then added, "I don't understand why [the police are] going back to [something that happened] in 1970, forty-six years ago."

In Egley's mind, he'd gotten away with murder for nearly half a century, and for him, it just seemed like there wasn't a point in dealing with this now, all these years later.

Egley would be confronted in court for the first time with the details of the murder he had committed. *Stabbing, strangulation, abrasions, contusions, rape,* and *blood* were just some of the words read directly from the medical examiner's report. His motive? Rejected sexual advances. The result? A violent, undeserved act on a helpless woman. Why had he done it? Had the years he'd lived as a free man erased the motive from his mind? So many questions that would never be answered to anyone's satisfaction because no reason could ever justify what Egley had done.

Before deciding on his sentence, the judge listened to the recommendations made by both Egley's side and the family of Loretta Jones.

The prosecution team consisted of Carbon County Attorney Gene Strate, Deputy County Attorney Jeremy Humes, Assistant Attorney General Gregory Ferbrache, Shelley Coudreaut, and Russell Smith. Mr. David Allred represented the defendant, and the Honorable Judge George Harmond Jr. presided.

Strate approached the bench after making slight changes to the presentence details. He presented the judge with case photographs and called his attention to one photo of Loretta Jones at age twenty-three, sitting strong and tall, young and smiling. Mr. Strate pointed out that she was a small woman, five-foot-six inches and 135 pounds, as noted in the medical examiner's report. The other photos viewed weren't as innocent; murder scenes never are.

"As Mr. Egley sits here now, he's obviously elderly, quite frail. But he wasn't always a frail man," Strate said. "Mr. Egley, at the time of the murder, was thirty years of age and was obviously a big strapping man. Mr. Egley was healthy, strong, and young. Far stronger than Miss Jones."

Another photograph was shown to the court. Taken at the time of Mr. Egley's 1970 court date, it displayed Egley being escorted to court by Price City Police Chief Art Poloni.

The original hearing was summarized for the court.

In 1970, Egley was charged with the crime and taken into custody. However, the court took the preliminary hearing under advisement, and Judge Tom G. Platis ruled that there was insufficient evidence to bind Mr. Egley over, and they released him.

Mr. Strate continued. "The result left Loretta's family in an awful state of limbo that went on for nearly half a century."

The county attorney shared how Heidi grew up without a mother and how Loretta's absence scarred not only her childhood but the entire family. At one point, he even implied that Heidi's grandfather, Parley, had died prematurely because he'd lost his daughter.

He thanked those involved in bringing the cold case to justice but added, "This could have all been alleviated years ago if Mr. Egley had just taken responsibility for his action. But the simple truth of the matter is, Your Honor, that Mr. Egley has spent the best years of his life as a free man, going about his own affairs, going about his own business and personal activities. He's had no real consequences for this heinous crime."

In 1970, first-degree murder (UCA 76-30-4) was a capital crime punishable by death. Also, in 1970, murder in the second degree, which is what Mr. Egley was facing, says the following: Every person guilty of murder in the second degree shall be imprisoned at hard labor in the state prison for a term, which shall not be less than ten years in which may be for life.

Mr. Strate closed by asserting, "So the state is recommending the sentence, Your Honor, of ten years to life for Mr. Egley."

The attorney general's representative, Mr. Ferbrache, agreed with the state's recommended sentence but added two additional points. One: he was grateful that the defendant had ultimately taken responsibility for the murder, sparing the family the rigor of going through a trial.

And two: "Forty-six years does not mitigate the heinousness or the brutality of the defendant's act, and for the crime of murder, the defendant deserves to go to prison consistent with those murderers who are caught at or near the time the crime was committed and whose admission, in this case, was only on the heels of Deputy Brewer's investigation."

Although Heidi had seen Tom Egley on the prior court video hearing, today she would finally have her turn to stand in the same room and address the man who had murdered her mother in cold blood.

Heidi stood before the court, before her friends and family, and all those who had supported her and helped her get to this point, and yet she looked at none of them. She saw only Tom Egley.

She'd planned the words she wanted to say to him and had thought about them for most of her life. Finally, after all this time, Heidi Jones-Asay was rewarded with an emotional moment she often doubted would come to fruition.

Standing before Thomas Edward Egley, Heidi found the courage and the will to confront the man who had murdered her mother and ripped a life of memories and love from her.

> *On the morning of July 31, 1970, I opened my bedroom door to find my lifeless mother, Loretta Marie Jones, lying on the floor in a pool of blood. She had been stabbed not once, not twice, but more than seventeen times. Her clothes had been cut off of her.*
>
> *She had been raped, and her throat was slit. I was in shock and terrified, and all alone. That day my life changed forever. I no longer had the one person in the world that would protect me and who loved me unconditionally. My mom was taken away from me by the selfish acts of one man.*
>
> *My mom was my hero that terrible night. She never screamed nor made a sound. She did everything she had to do to prevent me from coming out of my room.*
>
> *How does that make you feel, Tom Egley, knowing you left a four-year-old little girl all alone in the next room to find her mother's bloody and lifeless body?*
>
> *My mom was not there to comfort me from the repeated nightmares after that horrible night. I never felt safe again, especially at night. Every night I would double-check to*

make sure my grandparents locked the doors before going to bed. I was afraid Tom would come back and kill me or another member of my family. I continually looked over my shoulders to make sure Tom Egley was never there. I continued to look over my shoulder for many years.

I could not celebrate my mom's twenty-fourth birthday or any other birthday with her. We didn't get to eat cake, blow out candles, or open presents. She was not there to bake me a cake on my fifth birthday or my twenty-fifth. The last birthday cake I ever got from my mom was when I turned four. Birthdays, Mother's Day, Thanksgiving, and Christmas were always celebrated by a stop at the Elmo city cemetery to place flowers and shed a tear at my mom's grave.

Tom Egley took my mom away from me. My mom was not there for my first crush, my first kiss, my first date, my first heartbreak, my first dance, getting my driver's license, my high school graduation, or my first car. She wasn't there to help me pick a wedding dress or even attend my wedding.

My mom was not there for any milestones in my life. I missed out on every mommy-daughter moment. The pain, the stress, and the nightmare my grandparents lived with from having their beautiful, beautiful daughter brutally raped in her own home was more than any parent should have to endure. My grandfather's heart was broken, and his life was cut short due to a heart attack, a heart attack that did not need to happen had his daughter not been so brutally murdered.

Tom Egley took not only my mother, but also a daughter, a granddaughter, a sister, an aunt, and a niece away *from my family. He took a friend, a sweet, kind, and loving young woman, from this world at the age of twenty-three.*

I always knew the name and the face of the man who killed my mom. I always knew it was Tom. In 1989, I began looking for justice for my mom and never stopped even after hitting the brick walls. I knew one day I would see Tom again. Once I found Detective Brewer, who believed in getting justice for my mom as much as I did, I knew the date [I would see Tom Egley again] would be in court.

When my mom's body was exhumed, and the word of the exhumation had spread like wildfire to Rocky Ford, Colorado, I knew then that Tom would be squirming. I was ecstatic to hear [the news]. Tom confessed. Finally, I was relieved when he was arrested and transported to the Carbon County jail. I am angry that Tom did not stand trial in 1970 for my mother's murder. I am angry that Tom lived a life outside of prison.

I always wanted Tom's children and grandchildren to know what kind of a monster he is and for what he did forty-six years ago to a single mom when she was twenty-three years old. Tom Egley is a poor excuse for a human being.

As a child, there was no counseling to help deal with the trauma and loss of my mom. In my adult years, I searched for psychiatrists, psychologists, and counselors to help with my loss and abandonment issues. After forty-six years, I still celebrate my mother's birthday, Mother's Day, Thanksgiving, and Christmas with a stop at the Elmo city cemetery to place a flower and shed a tear at her grave.

From this day forward that tear shed will be a happy tear, for it will be that we're finally getting justice for my

mom. I believe that even though my mom is not here phys-
ically, her spirit lives on. I believe it was her spirit that
helped orchestrate all the chance meetings and events that
led to the confession and the arrest of Tom Egley. After
forty-six years, it was time.

My hope for Tom Egley is for him to be sentenced to
prison for the rest of his life. I hope he will take his last and
final breath behind prison bars. All alone, not holding the
hand of a loved one. I hope that the remainder of Tom's life
is lonely and a living hell. If Tom is eligible for parole, I
will be at the parole hearing to ensure he never walks as a
free man again. Thank you.

Heidi returned to her seat. Despite the emotional toll, she felt empowered in confronting the perpetrator, even though lingering feelings of anxiety and sadness accompanied it. Later, she would ruminate on how Tom had avoided eye contact the entire time she spoke. It had been hard to look at him, but she was grateful she'd had the courage and support to do so.

"It was gut-wrenching to hear his voice talk so noncha-lantly." She shared with Sgt. Brewer that she hadn't prepared herself to see Tom in the flesh, not just because of what he had done but also because of how he had aged.

Tom Egley was now a frail old man who used glasses to read and took a while to find his voice when talking. He walked with hunched shoulders and moved slowly.

"I expected a monster, but he was just an old man," Heidi said after first seeing him.

Even so, his hands, bony and sun-spotted, were the same ones that had slid a knife into Loretta Jones and removed her soul from this earth.

"Even monsters grow old, Heidi," was Brewer's answer.

The judge then moved on to Mr. Egley's attorney, Mr. Allred.

After meeting with the defendant, Allred felt the state's declaration regarding Mr. Egley's lack of remorse was incorrect. He then read from a statement that his client had provided earlier.

Allred stood and read Egley's statement: "I didn't know that her daughter was there because I never did see her. I thought Loretta was home by herself. I'm sorry that she had to find her mother like that—more than she'll ever know. I'm terribly sorry with all my heart for taking her mother away from her. When I say I don't remember, I just don't after forty-six years. I've been as honest as I can be."

The reasoning behind Egley's insistence that he was unaware of Heidi's presence in the house was unclear. Perhaps he wanted to paint himself in a better light, implying he wouldn't have killed a child's mother if he'd known she was in the house.

Of course, Egley had told Karen Cox the opposite. He said he had known Heidi was home that night because Loretta had told him to be quiet during their argument so they wouldn't wake Heidi.

Either way, Allred continued, insisting that Egley felt remorse for the crime and expressed sorrow for what had occurred.

Perhaps it was only a lapse in an old man's memory, but one thing was sure, it seemed less like Egley was sorry for killing Loretta and more like he was sorry for getting caught. Bent over and fiddling with his chains, Tom awaited his sentence.

CHAPTER 35

Sentencing

Egley didn't address the judge further except to say he was
not satisfied with being sentenced to the Utah State Prison
in Bluffdale. He indicated that he would prefer to be held in
a facility closer to his home in Colorado so that family or friends
could visit him more easily. But 7th District Judge George Harmond waved off his request, explaining that correction officials
would make such a decision and that it was out of his hands.

All parties rested, and the judge ordered the defendant to
stand. With some difficulty and a slight tremble in his bones,
Thomas Egley rose from his chair and stood before the court.
The judge asked if he wished to make a statement. His attorney,
Mr. Allred, indicated that the defendant wanted the court to
know that the words he'd just read were Tom's feelings today,
and there was nothing more he wished to add.

A distinct tension hung heavy in the air, suffocating the
room with anticipation. Heidi, her heart heavy with the weight
of four and a half decades of unanswered questions and unresolved grief, sat barely able to breathe, her hand clenched

tightly in Kevin's. Beside her, Sgt. Brewer, the detective who had tirelessly pursued justice for the young mother's senseless murder, exuded a quiet determination, his gaze unwavering as he awaited the sentencing. Throughout the courtroom, family members and supporters of the victim shared in the collective anxiety, their eyes flickering with a mixture of hope and trepidation as the judge prepared to deliver the final sentence.

There were no objections to imposing the prison term on this date, but before Judge Harmond handed down the conviction, he looked directly at Tom Egley and spoke in a level voice.

"I'm unsure what it would take to drive one human being to do this to another human being. It's unclear to the court how a man can live with this on his mind and on his conscience for forty years. And lastly, it's unclear to the court whether or not you really feel remorse for what you've done."

For the first time, Egley spoke up, his voice quiet and weak. "I've always felt remorse," he uttered.

Judge Harmond continued. "Well, I don't know whether you actually feel remorse or not, because it's been so long that this has gone by. You've lived your life as if nothing happened. So all I can judge by is your actions. That's all I can use."

And after waiting forty-six years, the sentencing hearing was over in thirty-two minutes. Judge Hammond sentenced Thomas Edward Egley under the 1970 version of the criminal code to an indeterminate term of ten years to life in the Utah State Prison. Heidi received a letter from the parole board much later indicating that Tom would come up for parole in twenty years; however, his attorney, David Allred, said this case would not be eligible for an appeal.

At seventy-six and not in the greatest health, it was unlikely that Tom would live beyond the minimum sentence of ten years. Although Tom had lived more years on the outside than he would on the inside, it was likely he would die behind bars.

Outside the courthouse, news teams from Salt Lake City gathered statements from those who had spoken in court.

Carbon County Attorney Gene Strate told KSL news: "The community of Carbon County has been seeking justice for Loretta's brutal murder for a very long time, particularly the victim's daughter, who was four years old when she discovered her mother's body. The defendant's prison sentence brings solace in knowing that Loretta Jones's family will have the justice they rightly deserve. Sergeant Brewer and Detective Hendricks from the Carbon County Sheriff's Office should be commended for their efforts."

Attorney Sean Reyes chimed in. "We're grateful that Sgt. Brewer was willing to reopen the case and for the excellent work by the Carbon County investigators to solve this forty-six-year-old murder. After a lifetime of uncertainty, I am hopeful that this conviction and sentence to prison brings some measure of closure to those who have suffered the most from her loss."

ABC4 asked Heidi if she had been hoping that the defendant would speak in a meaningful way or say something other than what he said. "I was hoping he would have turned and told me he was sorry for killing my mom. That's what I was really hoping for."

However, it didn't change the relief and the ending to what she'd spent the majority of her life thinking would never happen. "I'm back to being ecstatic," Heidi said. "Tom is going to prison for the rest of his life. He got ten years, and to me that's a life sentence."

For Sgt. Brewer, this was a career-defining moment. The conviction was the culmination of nearly seven years of dedicated investigation on the cold case by Carbon County investigators, almost forty-six years after the events occurred. Obtaining a confession from a suspect for any cold case took serious work, but especially one almost five decades old. And yet this was more than just a job for Sgt. Brewer. This was something he'd dedicated his heart to, and he was as connected to the outcome of the case as the woman who'd first gotten him involved.

"I had to pinch myself a little bit," Sgt. Brewer said after the sentencing hearing. "I choked up a little bit, especially during Heidi's statement. It was pretty powerful."

Back at his office, Sgt. Brewer was taken aback when the words *I owe you an apology* appeared on his computer screen. The email came from Judge Elayne Storrs, a luminary in the judicial landscape who had retired in 2014. She left behind a legacy from her tenure in the Utah 7th Judicial District and with both the Carbon County and Wellington Justice Courts.

LuDeen was familiar with Elayne as her visiting teacher and respectfully referred to her as "Sister Storrs." In the LDS community, a visiting teacher is a devout woman tasked with supporting and guiding other women within the church boundaries, known as the ward. This role is coordinated through the Relief Society, and typically, two visiting teachers are paired with each woman, ensuring regular monthly contact to deliver spiritual messages and offer assistance.

During these routine visits, LuDeen openly shared her deep trust in and respect for Sgt. Brewer. It was through these heartfelt conversations that Sister Storrs learned of LuDeen's unwavering faith in the detective's dedication and integrity.

With a remarkable sense of humility and introspection, Judge Storrs reached out to Sgt. Brewer. She candidly acknowledged that the political backdrop influenced her earlier hesitations, particularly Sheriff James Cordova's reelection year. Many suspected the case was being revived primarily for political gain. However, setting aside those past reservations, Judge Storrs conveyed her appreciation for Brewer's relentless belief in the case and his pursuit of justice.

For Brewer, receiving such a vote of confidence from the esteemed judge was a profound affirmation, offering solace to a detective often navigating the challenges of under-recognition.

———

As Heidi Jones-Asay settled in with the knowledge that Tom would never see another day as a free man, she sat back in awe of everything and everyone who had contributed to getting to this day. For Heidi, the day of Tom Egley's arrest was surreal, a moment she'd waited for, one she'd dreamed about, and one she often thought wouldn't happen. Ultimately, it was because of Heidi's dedication and her refusal to give up that Tom Egley had finally ended up where he belonged.

CHAPTER 36

LIFE IN PRISON

U tah State Correctional Facility (USCF) features floor-to-ceiling windows in numerous housing sections, allowing those housed there to enjoy natural light and views of the surrounding mountains. This view is a far cry from the old Draper facility that held prisoners for seventy years. One billion dollars was spent to open the new prison in 2022. The two-hundred-acre compound was moved five miles west of Salt Lake City and currently houses 2,400 inmates.

Tom's last steps on the outside were walking from a patrol car to inside a barbed-wire fence. He spent his first six years of incarceration at the crumbling "Point of the Mountain" facility. Like every other convicted criminal going inside for the first time, he was given an Inmate Orientation Handbook. Soon after, he was evaluated for risk, skills, and health needs. Tom was assigned Level 3, which allowed inmates to leave their cells but remain inside the compound.

The old prison lacked adequate space for treatment, rehabilitation, education, and job-training programs. It was dark and overcrowded, according to correctional officers. Tom's new building, Currant (like the berry), houses geriatric, ADA, and medically dependent inmates. The new prison "complex," as corrections officials define it, will have bigger classrooms and libraries—including a family-history library—seven nondenominational chapels, music rooms, computer labs, gymnasiums, recreation yards, and even barbershops.

Sharing a single cell that included a bunk bed, a desk, and a toilet is a thing of the past. Tom is housed in either a cubicle-style living area that gives inmates more space to move around or a cell with eight bunks, including a toilet and shower with some privacy. "The inmates earn what they get. We house inmates according to their behavior in prison. If they behave well, they can buy more commissary, they have more visits, they can have more time on the phone, more calls," Officer Turley said in an interview with KSL news.

It is unsure as to how Tom spends his day. Perhaps he plays cards, watches TV, or indulges in the true crime novels or detective magazines that once held his interest. It is doubtful that he would take advantage of educational opportunities, skill-based programs, or even mental health therapy. Tom has cancer. It is unknown if the cause is the result of him being a heavy smoker for most of his life or from another reason. He stands stooped over, and his fading blue eyes have cataracts. He is probably one of the many inmates who stand in the "pill line" twice a day to receive medication.

An interesting article, "Too Nice for Inmates or Redefined?" by Pat Reavy, KSL.com, posted July 25, 2022, features a photo of the medical and mental health unit in the new complex. Blue, teal, and sea-green chairs circle a nice oak coffee table, and sunlight streams in from high glass windows, giving the room a sense of cozy warmth even though the floor is concrete and the walls are cinder block.

Perhaps Egley finds consolation in the plush, cushioned chairs and the well-lit space.

But if Tom's prior behavior is any indication, it's unlikely that he will form connections with fellow inmates or receive outside visitors. The injustice lies in the fact that he got to live the prime years of his life in freedom, while Loretta's best years were spent in the grave and Heidi's were consumed by the relentless search for her mother's killer. He deserves every day of his incarceration. But in some ways, it doesn't feel like justice at all.

In 2017, the year after he was arrested and sentenced, Tom Egley attempted to appeal his conviction. He contended that he was entrapped into confessing, that too much time had passed since the commission of the crime, that he should've been tried in Colorado, where he lived, and that he wasn't allowed to have witnesses appear on his behalf. The court assigned Price, Utah, lawyer Don Torgerson to present Egley's case. However, after Torgerson studied the case records, he concluded the appeal would be frivolous and filed a motion to withdraw from the proceeding. After that, Egley no longer pursued an appeal.

As with any true crime story, the more complete information that can fill the pages of a book, the better, so several attempts to contact Mr. Egley by mail were made in the hopes of obtaining his life story directly from him.

After many months of writing, a single envelope with the Utah State Prison return address appeared by mail.

In blue ink on white lined paper, in very neat handwriting, it read short and to the point:

Hi Shawnee

I received your last two letters and I am responding.

First, I do not want any visits, Thanks. You are not on my visiting list.

Second, I have not been writing to Karen Cox*!! [She maintained this.]

Third I am not interested in sharing my life story!!

Fourth — Please don't write again,

Sincerely Tom Egley

While transporting Tom from Salt Lake to the Carbon County jail, Tom opened up to Sgt. Brewer a bit. Brewer always carried a pack of cigarettes in his vehicle "to relax the suspect and get them talking." So after they stopped for a cigarette break, Tom "jabber-jawed" from the back seat with the story about how he was kicked out of the Navy. Tom had been guarding an old aviation area and fell asleep. Two other Navy guys saw that he was sleeping and took his rifle. When he awoke and noticed it was gone, he had to explain it to his commanding officer and was discharged from his position.

Brewer recounted that during the transport to the prison following Tom's conviction, an eerie silence hung heavy in the air — Tom didn't utter a single word.

CHAPTER 37

No Such Thing as Closure

S o when had Tom's daughter Mary learned that her father was a murderer? She and her mother, Marsha, had a weekly date to drive about an hour from where they lived to play bingo. They were close and talked about most things, but about ten years ago, they were driving to another bingo day when Marsha dropped a bomb on her. "Mary, there is something I need to tell you." Never in a million years did she think she would hear what her mother told her, that while they were living in Helper, her father, Tom, was accused of murder and that Marsha believed he did it. She told Mary she had finally left Tom much later because she had feared him. This news hit Mary hard, and she tried to connect Tom's actions to the father she knew. Upon reflection, she realized that this was why he probably didn't want anything to do with her; weirdly, it made her feel better. She could stop blaming herself for thinking she had done something to cause his absence. When her mother told her this, Tom had not been arrested yet. "The hardest part for me as an adult," Mary said, "was when they convicted him, and it appeared in the Rocky Ford newspaper. All my family still live in Colorado and were blasting it on Facebook. I got lots of calls about it." It was painful and confusing.

Mary has watched the TV documentaries made about the murder and said she can make it through some of them, and others make her sick to her stomach. She finds it inequitable that none of the Egley children were interviewed to learn how Tom's actions have affected their lives. Definitely not on the scale that it has affected Heidi, but learning her father is a murderer is a heavy load to carry. "My heart goes out to Heidi, and I pray for her daily," Mary said.

When asked if Mary has any plans to contact her father or visit him, she said with a raspy voice, "When I learned that he was trying to get his prison stay transferred to Colorado because he said he wanted to be closer to family so they could visit him, I laughed. 'What freakin' family? What kid wants to visit you in prison when you killed somebody?'" Mary took a deep breath and meekly added, "I will not visit him because I am ashamed of him. I looked up to that man when I was little; he was my knight in shining armor, my hero, and so handsome. Now to know that he did that . . . He is a monster. I wished they would have got him right away because who knows how many people he has done this to because he moved around so much."

As far as Lauren, Tom's oldest daughter, is concerned, "Somebody like him is not worth the air we breathe. Let's hope he dies in there." Lauren said she felt compelled to reach out to Heidi when she heard about the murder and hoped to make the trip to Utah and meet her someday. She wished her peace.

Even within the Jones family, there were dissenting voices regarding the exhumation, TV documentaries, and the idea of a book about Loretta's murder. Some believed that Loretta should be allowed to rest in peace, viewing these actions as disruptive to her memory. Each individual's sentiment was deeply personal, and they had the right to express their concerns.

Yet Carolyn, Lila, and Bryon grasped the necessity of Heidi exhuming her mother's body. It was a desperate measure, perhaps the only avenue left to unravel the mystery, and it ignited a glimmer of hope for closure. However, standing by that open grave plunged them all back into the raw emotions of that tragic night and stirred up poignant memories. It was hard.

Carolyn said she doesn't like the word *closure*, as it never comes. "I told Heidi and Sgt. Brewer, when they were getting deep into the case, that even after you find the murderer, it isn't going to give you closure. It might bring answers, but it will never bring my sister back." Carolyn described it as having a filing cabinet in your brain where folders are labeled with different aspects of Loretta's murder—death, funeral, exhumation, etc. You keep trying to put them back to heal, but then here comes something else—the preliminary hearing or a news article—so you are forced to reopen the cabinet.

For David Brewer, closure meant he would have time to enjoy gaming again. "Not a day went by that this case didn't consume my mind," Brewer confessed as he finally stamped the red letters *CLOSED* on the thick, heavy, cold case file. It had been a constant presence in his life for seven years, affecting every aspect. Now he was eager to return to things he had not been able to enjoy for a long time.

Dating back to the 1980s, he began, like most, playing *Pac-Man* and *Asteroids* at local arcades with friends. His passion grew when games became available on home computers, leading him to play at least three times a week, mainly on his days off—Friday, Saturday, and Sunday. Gaming became an event that kept him up late into the night. As a Star Wars fanatic, he gravitated toward games of that genre, such as *Jedi*, *Fallout*, and *Fortnite*. "Gaming is the best stress reliever there is," Brewer remarked with a boyish grin. Now he enjoys playing with his kids, marveling at their skills despite their young age.

Closure is that fanciful word that we try to attain in hopes that our days of pain and suffering are over. The idea of closure seems to be totally unaware of the reality of the grieving process and that healing isn't a linear process where you suddenly get over a hurdle and everything is fine. The best one can hope for in reaching "closure" is the attainment of peace, understanding, and release that accompanies accepting the end of a relationship. *Acceptance* might be a better word than *closure* because it doesn't deny that our deceased loved ones still have an important place in our lives.

Knowing the whereabouts of her mother's body offered a better ending than many unsolved cases. Without a body or a grave, closure often feels elusive. Heidi had those elements, and they provided a sense of conclusion, plus the fact that her murderer had been held accountable and was spending his life in prison.

For Heidi, closure meant justice.

CHAPTER 38

On Air

*THE STORY OF LORETTA JONES' COLD CASE GEN-
ERATES NATIONAL EXPOSURE* "The cold case story of
Loretta Jones will be highlighted on March 18 on the Investigation Discovery channel's On the Case with Paula Zahn. The
program will explain how the victim's daughter, Heidi Jones-
Asay, pushed detectives to get answers and solve the 1970
murder of her mother." KOAL Broadcasting, March 13, 2018.

The filming for Paula Zahn unfolded in New York City, with
the ID Channel covering the expenses for Heidi, David,
Lori Kulow, and her brother, Jim. However, a challenge
emerged—Detective Brewer had a fear of flying. Two turbulent
experiences at thirty thousand feet had left him shaken, and he
vowed to keep his feet firmly anchored to the ground.

As a solution, he and his wife embarked on a road trip to
Pittsburgh and then opted for Amtrak to complete the journey
to NYC. Heidi and Kevin enjoyed their flight, and they all appreciated the hotel rooms.

Brewer remembered being extremely nervous when meeting Paula Zahn, who is not only very attractive but personable as well. Before the cameras rolled, makeup artists and lighting crews gave the guests movie-star treatment. The entire experience was positive for all of them despite the subject of the interviews being murder.

Together, the cold case duo would sit in front of four more documentary cameras, all filmed from locations in Price. "I spent five hours interviewing for twenty minutes of airtime," Brewer recalled. "They skip all the good case stuff," he added, smiling. "That is why we need a book."

Carolyn, Loretta's younger sister, also made the decision to speak with Paula Zahn in 2018. "I don't think I would do it again," she said after the fact. "When I did this [TV filming], I felt it would be therapeutic for me. But instead, I talked with them by phone for over two hours, and I had a total breakdown."

She also interviewed for A&E and said that after being on camera for over three hours, they only showed two to three minutes of her interview, and she felt much was left out. However, she liked the producer, Graham, who took the time to learn about Loretta as a person, not just a murder victim.

Due to the extensive news coverage, Tom's face became highly recognizable. During Brewer's escort to the Salt Lake prison, they made a midway stop at Chappy's in Spanish Fork for a bathroom break. As they were leading the handcuffed prisoner back to the car, a man exclaimed, "Hey, I recognize that guy [Tom] from TV." The onlooker took a few photos and later shared them on his Facebook page.

In the years since Egley's conviction, Heidi Jones-Asay has continued talking about the case and has appeared on numerous documentaries and podcasts. Her message to viewers and listeners is never to give up whatever you are pursuing. She also maintains a website, Justice for Loretta, that updates readers on her journey. In one comment, she wrote:

"As 2022 comes to an end, I just want to thank my new supporters, friends, and family. 2022 was a busy year. Our Episode on Cold Case Files premiered, and it was an incredible episode. Our story made it to the UK in Take A Break Magazine. And we did an interview with the number-one podcast, Morbid. We also did an episode with a new podcast, Whine Time, and got picked up in Taiwan for their True Crime podcast.

"Thank you for all your love, support and encouragement all these years! Never, ever give up! And as long as you have HOPE, you have a chance."

CHAPTER 39

MORE NAY THAN YEA

Noun: naysayer: a person who criticizes, objects to, or opposes something.

There were many more naysayers than supporters," reported Sgt. Brewer, who was realistically aware that many people didn't believe *he* could solve Loretta's case. Neither did they believe it could be solved at all, nor did they think that it should be taking up law enforcement time and taxpayers' money. After all, it happened in 1970. Let Loretta rest in peace. But what about Heidi's peace and the injustice of it all? Even his own department doubted him. He withstood comments both to his face and behind his back.

Sheriff Wood affirmed Detective Brewer's suspicions when he disclosed that another officer had questioned the intensity of their efforts on the case, wondering why they were dedicating so much attention to a cold case. To this, both Brewer and Wood responded, emphasizing that a life was taken, and the pursuit of justice for the murderer remained just as crucial today as it was in 1970. It's a homicide case, irrespective of its temperature. Although Brewer never discovered the identity of the ignorant individual who made the insensitive comment, the memory of it lingered.

There were times when his colleagues even taunted him, and few congratulated him when the case was solved. "They call it professional jealousy," Brewer stated nonchalantly, but the sting showed through his tough-guy facade.

From the moment Wood pinned on his sheriff badge, he gave Brewer the green light and supported him for the entire seven years. "I always believed David would eventually gather what he needed to crack the case. He never neglected his other responsibilities, yet he remained steadfast in his pursuit," said the sheriff, reflecting on the detective's dedication.

Dr. Rachel Walton and Sheriff Jeff Wood were more than just supporters; they were like strong pillars for Sgt. Brewer. When doubts or challenges arose, Dr. Walton's expertise and insights helped clear things up, and Sheriff Wood's leadership and encouragement gave Brewer a solid base. They didn't just sit on the sidelines; they actively cheered him on, reminding him of his strengths, celebrating small wins, and standing with him during tough times. In the harsh world of investigations, having such steady advocates really mattered. They turned moments of uncertainty into chances for Brewer to grow and keep going.

Brewer also credited Chief Deputy Cletis Steele, who stood steadfastly beside the sheriff and provided unwavering support for Brewer's endeavors to crack the case.

The cold case reignited Brewer's passion for hard investigative activity, and he worked on two other cold cases during his tenure with the sheriff's office. Unfortunately, he was unable to close those cases before he retired in 2023. "The bad thing about opening an old case is that there are so many that you can't solve, leaving those families unhappy and frustrated. Each case has its challenges, and some will never be solved."

Regarding Loretta's case, he added, "Working with Heidi was integral in solving her mother's case." Since he still doesn't believe in luck, he credits hard work and perseverance.

EPILOGUE

DAVID BREWER

"One of my heroes retired today. He is one of the best guys I know. Thanks for your service to the community. But more importantly to me, thanks for believing enough not to give up on a forty-six-year-old Cold Case! Thanks for fighting for my Mom and helping send the Boogeyman to prison.

Some heroes wear capes . . . mine wear Kevlar!"

Heidi posted this on her Justice for Loretta Facebook page, along with photos of Brewer accepting his retirement plaque from Sheriff Jeff Wood in April 2023.

Next to his retirement plaque hangs the Medal of Valor award bestowed upon Brewer in 2006. "I'm deeply honored to receive this award, as it stands as one of law enforcement's highest distinctions," Brewer remarked with pride. The Medal of Valor is reserved for officers who have displayed exceptional courage in the face of imminent danger, demonstrating extraordinary bravery in their actions.

"Jayden Seal, one year old, was swept away when a twenty-foot wall of water hit the Ford Bronco he and his family were riding in near Garley's Canyon, eleven miles north of Price. His brother, five-year-old Levi, died, and his two-year-old sister, Brooklynn, suffered non-life-threatening injuries. The family was on a Sunday night drive on a dirt road they had driven on hundreds of times in the past. They were crossing the wash when the wall of water hit their vehicle without warning. The Ford Bronco was swept along by the rushing water and kept bouncing off the sides of the canyon." (August 4, 2006—*Deseret News*)

Sgt. Tory Christiansen received an urgent call regarding a family trapped in a flash flood near Consumer Road. Brewer recalled his initial skepticism. "Is that location correct? There is no river there." But their disbelief turned to grim reality upon arrival.

A ferocious torrent surged through the barren desert landscape, carving fresh channels through the ancient wash. "My babies, my babies," came the desperate cries from a woman pointing downstream, directing them to the heart of the crisis. While Sgt. Christiansen opted for higher ground, Brewer dashed downstream, where he was met with a harrowing scene: a man cradling a limp child and a Ford Bronco stranded across the surging waters. Swiftly shedding their gear, Sgt. Christiansen and Brewer plunged into the rushing current. Brewer clung desperately to the Bronco, his feet struggling to find purchase against the relentless flow as he dug silt and mud out from the window. Despite their valiant efforts and the subsequent arrival of Life Flight, they could only recover the body of a five-year-old boy from the submerged vehicle. Undeterred, they persisted in their search for one-year-old Jayden. Despite exhaustive efforts and the assistance of cadaver dogs, the toddler was never found. Sgt. Christiansen also received the Medal of Valor.

Sgt. David Brewer worked for the Carbon County Sheriff's Office for twenty-one years, and now he was unpinning his badge and locking up his Glock 22. He and his wife welcomed a son to their family in 2018, and it was decided that they would move back east to be closer to his wife's family. "It will be nice to be in a place where no one knows I was a law enforcement officer," he said. However, there were several people in his new town who recognized him from the TV documentary series. "Hey, didn't I see you on TV?" or "Aren't you that guy who solved that cold case?" He doesn't mind a bit of notoriety, as he is very proud of his accomplishments in Utah. He wouldn't mind if the book afforded him a few opportunities to speak at his local bookstore or library.

Before he left Utah, David, who had a talent for woodworking, made challenge-coin boards for some of his colleagues at the sheriff's office. Each board, varying in size, needed to be lathed, sanded, and stained. Looking somewhat like an American flag, the boards have "shelf" lines that hold challenge coins. He paints a "thin blue line" on some to represent law enforcement, red for firefighters, and camo for the military. In the blue corner, he uses vinyl to add stars and the badges of the officer or military patch in the center. For challenge coin collectors, these can be hung on the wall or placed on a bookshelf at work or at home to signify their membership within a certain group of like-minded collectors.

Challenge coins are small, medallion-like tokens often adorned with the emblem or insignia of the presenting organization. Being given a challenge coin represents unity and honors the actions of those who receive it. They are collected by officers, firefighters, and military personnel.

Brewer enjoyed making the coin boards so much for his friends that he started Brewer's Workshop. This new passion gave him an outlet to showcase his talents in retirement, and he takes orders from all over the world. "I really enjoy making the boards and seeing all the different badges and patches," he said.

Through his military service and his tenure as a law enforcement officer, he has demonstrated unwavering dedication and commitment to his country and community. Now it's time for him to give back to his family.

HEIDI JONES-ASAY

In an emotional gesture of justice and remembrance, Heidi fulfilled a pact she had made with Sgt. Brewer at the beginning of the case.

"Who's your favorite football team?" Heidi asked David while joining him at a local coffee shop. Heidi's usual was the white chocolate pistachio matcha tea and, for Brewer, coffee. Black.

"Raiders, of course!" was Brewer's emphatic reply.

She had learned early on through one of their many conversations that David was a Raiders (NFL football team) fan, so shortly after Tom finally confessed to killing her mom, Heidi employed her son-in-law, Jesse Lomeli, a talented freehand tattoo artist in Orange County, California, to create a tattoo that would honor her promise to her detective friend and her mother.

Heidi had told Brewer that if he solved the case, she would get a Raiders tattoo. And when Brewer called to tell her that Tom had confessed, she said, "Oh shit . . . I guess I've got to get a Raiders tattoo."

David laughed and said, "I forgot all about that!"

She proudly displays it on the left side of her left leg: a patch-eyed Raider clad in helmet in front of a shield and two swords. To its left, two delicate pale blue roses add a touch of contrast and elegance—blue roses for her mother.

Heidi had spent her lifetime searching for the person who murdered her mother. She had written letters, attended psychic events, pounded on the doors of the police department and the county attorney's office, and worked side by side with her ally, Brewer, to finally put the murderer behind bars. She had reached the summit of her goal. Now what?

After Egley was sentenced to life in prison, Heidi flew to New York for the Paula Zahn program, did four more TV shows, was featured on the Morbid Broadcast twice, and was interviewed countless times for magazines and newspapers. "Life hasn't stopped," she said. "I've been busy busy."

Heidi had transitioned from a child who was prohibited from discussing her mom's murder to a woman who sought to share her story with anyone she could assist. This shift brought her a sense of release and freedom.

Heidi hoped to reach out to others whose lives had also been touched by tragedy. "If somebody's hurting and needs a little hope, I will be there for whoever they may be. Maybe a little justice for Loretta Jones will help other people in other ways," Heidi said with a smile. "That's how I'll keep my mother's memory alive."

Heidi finds immense joy in caring for their granddaughter every chance she gets and dog-sitting for her brother, friends, and neighbors. Despite their busy schedules, she and Kevin still make time for motorcycle rides in the summer, and she enjoys family reunions and spending time with old friends as well as the new ones she has met throughout her journey. While in California, she developed a passion for creating art with gourds. "I'm a gourdaholic," she professed. She paints, wood burns, and crafts birdhouses from them and finds the process to be both enjoyable and relaxing.

Heidi's nightmares have vanished. No longer does she wander through the house in her dreams, haunted by visions of impending doom at the keyhole. "I don't have to look over my shoulder anymore. The ghosts are gone," she declared. Now only fond memories of her mother linger, bringing her solace and peace.

Many years after Loretta's passing, Heidi would uncover the identity of her biological father through the revelations brought about by DNA testing, only to be met with the cruel twist of fate that he had already passed away.

And although she never knew her real father, for four precious years, she had a mother. Just as Heidi's birth would change Loretta's life, Loretta's death would drastically alter the course of Heidi's, taking it in a direction Heidi herself never expected. Forty-six years after Loretta Jones's death, her daughter would help find her killer and finally bring him to justice; discovering closure, as it turned out, wasn't impossible after all. But justice was.

On March 16, 2024, Heidi was contacted by the Utah Department of Corrections, informing her that Inmate #229905, Thomas Egley, had passed away on 3/15/2024. He was eighty-three years old and had spent seven years and five months in prison. Per public policy FI14: the Department of Corrections disposes of the deceased inmate's body per any written directive from him or his family.

Tom Egley left no directives and was cremated by the prison.

SHAWNEE'S ACKNOWLEDGMENTS

Thanks a million times to Heidi and David for trusting me with the privilege of writing their remarkable tale. Their unwavering patience in answering my countless questions has been invaluable throughout this journey. It's been a pleasure getting to know you both.

I'm deeply grateful to my late mother, Sylvia Howard Nelson, whose writing talents I came to appreciate far too late. Her influence has shaped my writing abilities and many other talents and skills I possess today.

A special thank-you to my daughter, Shaffryn, whose meticulous reviews pushed me to new heights. Her dedication was steadfast, and her brutal honesty was always appreciated. She also shares my mother's writing talents, and I hope she'll consider channeling that gift into writing her own book. I assure her that I'll eagerly read and reread it, just as she did with mine.

I want to express my heartfelt appreciation and love to my life partner, Rob, for standing by me and providing constant support through all my "Squirrel" endeavors. I promise the next one will be easier.

I sincerely appreciate all of Loretta Jones's family members, Egley's daughters, and everyone connected to the case for entrusting me to share their stories.

To Professor Rachel Walton, whose own incredible story deserves to be written: thank you for your input and support.

To my legal counsel, Denise: thank you for patiently addressing all my questions, no matter how trivial.

Thank you to Matt from Reedsy, who did an excellent job with my first edit and set the book on the right path.

To Enchanted Ink: thank you for your amazing editing services.

And thanks to our dog, Sketch, who sat at my feet patiently waiting for a walk when I assured him it would happen after "just one more page."

Lastly, thanks to God for blessing me so abundantly!

HEIDI'S ACKNOWLEDGMENTS

I'd like to thank Sergeant David Brewer for believing the words of four-year-old Heidi as I relayed my story to him repeatedly. I told him every rumor and story about my mom's case. He took it to heart. When I say, "Some heroes wear capes, but mine wear Kevlar," I truly mean it.

Carbon County Sherriff's Office for all their hard work and dedication to my mom's cold case. The full support from Sheriff Jeff Wood and the time and support Detective Roger Taylor and Detective Wally Hendricks dedicated to her case was truly a blessing.

Deanna Fausett, crime victims' advocate with the Carbon County Sheriff's Office, for her wisdom and support.

Dr. Rachel Walton for researching and discovering my mom's case and for believing that it deserved to be investigated after so many years.

The Utah Attorney General's Office for stepping in and supporting the Carbon County District Attorney's Office.

Judge George Harmond for sentencing Egley to the fullest extent allowed by law.

Lori Kulow Fenner and Jim Kulow for reliving their nightmare of July 1970 and supporting me and law enforcement in getting justice.

Lisa Carter for your crucial assistance with the case.

My family for supporting me in getting my mom's case re-opened. I know that reliving the nightmare over and over again wasn't easy. Forty-six years was a long time to wait for justice.

My many friends who cheered me on from near and far. I love you all.

Thank you, Jo'Anne Smith, for your support like no other. The day I met you is forever engraved in my mind. The wisdom, love, and gifts that you share are pure love and light.

Thank you to those who didn't think I should reopen my mom's case. Your nonsupport made me want to do it even more. I learned to believe in the impossible.

My husband, Kevin Asay, who has been my love and support through it all—the sleepless nights, the nightmares, and all the tears, happy and sad. He stood by me and supported me like no other. I love you a million trillion more than twenty.

The support from the media, television, and podcasters: thank you for telling and sharing my story to give a little hope to someone out there who needs it. As long as there is hope, you have a chance.

Shawnee Barnes for taking on the task of writing our story. The writes, the rewrites, the edits, and more edits. Thank you for putting our words in black and white so we can finally have a book and share our story with the world.

And to four-year-old Heidi, we did it! We really did it!

DAVID'S ACKNOWLEDGMENTS

I extend my heartfelt gratitude to the remarkable individuals who were instrumental in assisting me with this seven-year investigation:

First and foremost, my wife, Brittany, whose unwavering support strengthened me throughout this challenging journey. Her belief in me and steadfast encouragement were key as we faced each hurdle together.

My father, Mark Brewer, deserves special recognition for the invaluable lessons he taught me about the value of hard work. His example was a guiding beacon, instilling in me a strong work ethic that propelled me forward, even in the most trying times.

The Jones family's support and patience were a source of comfort and encouragement, reminding me that I was not alone in this pursuit of justice.

Sheriff Jeff Wood and Chief Deputy Cletis Steele, I am deeply grateful for your solid support and trust in my judgment throughout this case. Your backing was instrumental in keeping me motivated and focused.

Detectives Roger Taylor, Wally Hendricks, and Dale Maxfield, thank you for your assistance with the case.

Rick Shaw, thank you for your extremely helpful assistance with the newspaper articles, helping to shed light on crucial aspects of the case.

I am indebted to the numerous witnesses whose interviews filled significant gaps and provided vital clues. Thank you for your cooperation and willingness to come forward.

To my esteemed professional colleagues, including Ed Span, Vince Meister, and Ben Pender, your wisdom and experience were critical resources throughout this challenging journey.

Dr. Rachel Walton, your friendship, advice, and steadfast support were a source of strength during the most difficult moments.

And a special thanks to Shawnee Barnes for transforming a chance meeting into a great book and a wonderful friendship.

Last but certainly not least, Heidi Jones-Asay, your unfaltering belief in me, your relentless push, and your tireless dedication to seeking justice for your mother were nothing short of inspiring. Your love and determination were the driving forces behind our shared commitment to seeing this case through to its rightful conclusion.

Shawnee's career began as a child abuse investigator with the State of Utah, advancing to become a trainer and supervisor. She also taught criminal justice as an adjunct professor and collaborated with law enforcement on complex cases statewide. Relocating to Colorado, Shawnee assumed the role of chief probation officer for the 9th Judicial District, managing three counties and a drug court. Shawnee holds two undergraduate degrees and a criminology certificate from the University of Utah. She began her writing journey in Ireland. Now settled in Colorado, she enjoys reading, traveling, quilting, and exploring the outdoors alongside her partner, Rob.

www.ingramcontent.com/pod-product-compliance
Lightning Source LLC
Chambersburg PA
CBHW022046020426
42335CB00012B/569